GW00693972

The Proof of the Pudding

Miles Bunday at two and a half years of age

The proof of the pudding

a collection of letters from parents and case studies of ADHD/Hyperactive children published to mark the 30th Anniversary of the Hyperactive Children's Support Group, 1977 - 2007.

Introduction by Sally Bunday, MBE
Founder & Secretary
of the HACSG

Foreword by Professor Neil Ward, BSc., MSc.(HONS), PhD.,
Senior Lecturer in Analytical Chemistry,
University of Surrey.

HACSG PUBLICATIONS

copyright © Hyperactive Children's Support Group, 2007
Produced for HACSG by Print Rite, Freeland, Witney OX29 8HX

*To Miles Bunday, who started it all,
and to his sisters, Lucy and Mandy,
who were always supportive;
to the late Vicky Colquhoun, honorary
Chairman of the HACSG for 23 years
and, last but certainly not least, to
all the parents, professionals and
supporters of the group
I dedicate this book.
- Sally Bunday*

Miles Bunday, left, age ten months, with sister Lucy

Foreword

by Professor Neil Ward, BSc., MSc.(HONS), PhD.,
Senior Lecturer in Analytical Chemistry, University of Surrey

For thirty years the Hyperactive Children's Support Group, which for a large part of its existence consisted of no more than its founder and director Sally Bunday and her mother, the late Vicky Colquhoun acting as honorary chairman, has offered free advice and practical assistance to thousands of families of hyperactive children. Many of these families in their turn formed support groups throughout the UK. The group came into existence when knowledge of hyperactivity was very limited and in many cases parents themselves were blamed for their children's "misbehaviour". The standard medical response was (and remains) the administration of medication and behavioural therapy, neither of which go beyond treating the symptoms of the disorder.

The basic message of the HACSG has been, and remains, quite simple: cut out artificial additives from the diet of your children (and some foodstuffs that may be causing problems, such as cow's milk). As the selection of parents' letters contained in this book clearly demonstrates, the nutritional approach to hyperactivity "works", and not only does it work, but it does quite frequently produce what can only be described as spectacular results. Many parents have witnessed a dramatic turnaround in the behaviour of their hyperactive children, passing from the unruly, aggressive and anti-social behaviours combined with sleeplessness and poor concentration that are the hallmarks of AD/HD to a behaviour approaching normality. The children sense the change in themselves and begin to enjoy being able to sit quietly and pay attention to what they are doing or participate in activities with their friends. Teachers who, like parents, have an intimate knowledge of the children under their care, are amongst the first to notice the changes and many parents comment that they feel that they have "got their children back" as well as their family life.

While the HACSG has steadfastly pursued its course and stuck to its founding principles, on the way helping with its own research to broaden our understanding of the disorder, the medical and scientific communities, have, for the most part, dismissed the case for the nutritional approach to AD/HD, usually describing the evidence provided by parents' and teachers' feed-back as purely "anecdotal". As incredible as it may seem, many a doctor still does not accept that a link exists between diet and behaviour. What we eat on a daily basis bears no relation, apparently, to how our brains and bodies function.

Whilst everybody these days accepts that the human organism, like any other living system, requires certain nutrients at certain levels in order to function, nutrients such as vitamins, minerals, essential fatty acids, etc - we ignore the fact that industrially produced food, food that is mass-produced in factories and contains a cocktail of artificial colours, flavours, flavour enhancers and preservatives, food which in many cases forms the basis of many young people's diets, is lacking in many of these essential nutrients and over time can have a disastrous effect on our health.

We know that the nervous system and brain function take years to fully develop after birth and that this development can be disrupted by chemical agents which the human organism is not designed to deal with, chemical agents such as PCBs which act as hormone disruptors, for example.**(1)** Recently published research has now established once and for all, that artificial additives, of which there is often a combination in packaged foods on the supermarket shelves cause behavioural disorders.**(2)**

Science has at long last caught up with our day to day experience. To many people it would seem a matter of common sense that the daily consumption of a diet consisting of "convenience" foods that are low in nutritional value and high in sugars, animal fats and artificial additives can only do harm in the long term. We know from our experience and from the experience of groups like the HACSG, that a poor quality diet leads to all kinds of health problems. We are, literally, what we eat. High and rising levels of obesity and diabetes, allergies, asthma, hyperactivity and autism to name but a few of the chronic ailments now afflicting both adults and children in the western world, are especially evident in those countries where packaged, processed and additive-laden food has for long been the standard diet.

The parents of hyperactive children who speak in these pages are not recounting anecdotes. They are relating truthfully their own, often painful, experience with a hyperactive child (or children) and how as families they struggled with and succeeded in overcoming the disorder, and how their children went on to lead normal and constructive lives. If we are looking for proof that the nutritional approach to hyperactivity has a sound basis, we need look no further than these pages. The proof of the pudding, as they say, is in the eating and for many, many parents and their hyperactive children, the nutritional approach of the HACSG has been a life-saver.

Notes

(1) According to a study undertaken for Greenpeace and the WWF-UK, hazardous chemicals that are used in a range of household products end up in the bodies of unborn children via the mother. This study confirmed the presence of known or suspected dangerous chemicals in umbilical cord blood. In a recent Guardian newspaper report (September 2, 2007) scientists from the Arctic Monitoring and Assessment Programme found high levels of man-made chemicals in the blood of pregnant Inuit women. Twice as many girls are being born as boys in some Arctic villages. The scientists measured the levels of chemicals in the women's blood that mimic hormones and concluded that they were capable of altering the sex of unborn babies.

(2) Research commissioned by the Food Standards Agency (FSA) and carried out at Southampton University. Published in the medical journal *The Lancet* (Sept.6, 2007) The findings support similar research done in 2000 (the Isle of Wight study) which showed a definite link between food additives and behavioural problems such as temper tantrums, poor concentration, hyperactivity and allergic reactions. In this latest study, the effect of a combination of artificial colourings and the preservative sodium benzoate that are used in the manufacture of sweets, drinks and processed foods in the UK, was tested on groups of 3-year-old and 8 to 9-year old children. One wonders how much more "scientific evidence" of a link between artificial food additives and human behaviour will be required before action is taken to ban their use, especially in "foods" aimed specifically at children. As has been noted on many occasions artificial colourings, flavourings and preservatives add nothing to the nutritional value of the items in question. Children themselves have become "hooked" on highly flavoured and attractive-looking "snacks" and drinks, making the job of parents and educators to switch children to healthy eating habits that much more difficult.

Miles with sister Lucy

Miles, age four, with cousin Jamie

Introduction

by Sally Bunday, MBE
Founder & Secretary of the HACSG

The HACSG (Hyperactive Children's Support Group), was founded in 1977, following the improvements in my son, diagnosed as severely hyperactive at the age of two and a half. He would have been diagnosed as ADHD had those terms been in existence in 1973-4.

In common with many children, as our research has shown, he suffered abnormal thirst, poor appetite (finicky), restlessness, Jekyll & Hyde mood changes, defiance, aggression, poor sleep, great strength, overheating, high pain threshold, night terrors and endless catarrh and sickness on feeds. Despite the diagnosis, no real help was offered.

Our breakthrough came from America and the late Dr Ben Feingold, who found that many children with symptoms like my son, could be aggravated by certain food additives and salicylates (an aspirin-like substance), that occurs naturally in items like orange, tomato, cola, blackcurrant, raisins (to name a few). As a family, we followed the Feingold Food Programme 100% and within a week there were substantial improvements. The catarrh cleared up (this in itself must make a child feel irritable), the thirst normalised, bedtimes and sleep were improved and mood swings decreased. The wild look in his eyes disappeared.

As the years went by and our work continued, it became clear that the biochemical, nutritional, allergy and food/chemical intolerance aspects were playing a considerable part in the behaviour of many children.

In 1981 we learned about the role of Essential Fatty Acids, how important they were in brain function, the immune system, eczema/asthma and the control of thirst.

The HACSG Honorary Chairman, the late Vicky Colquhoun met the late Dr. David Horrobin, a world expert on the value and importance of EFAs Omega6 and Omega3 in many conditions including depression and alcoholism. Many of the symptoms characteristic of hyperactivity were found to be similar to those found in Dr. Horrobin's research. With his help, the group undertook its own research into the role of Omega6 - evening primrose oil - and this led to the publication of *A Lack of Essential Fatty Acids As A Possible Cause of Hyperactivity* in 1981. EFA research around the world since has confirmed the early work. Current research has shown that Omega3 fatty acids DHA and EPA which are found in fish, flax and hemp oils, plus Omega6 DGLA, are more effective.

Countless children of all ages have since benefitted from nutritional supplements containing EFAs and certain co-factors (to assist metabolism of EFA's), i.e. B Vitamins, Vitamin C, Magnesium and Zinc.

Through the University of Surrey and Bio-Lab Medical Unit in London, tests have been done using hair, sweat and urine to discover if there are imbalances of minerals like zinc or raised toxic levels of metals like lead or aluminium. Very rarely do we find a child with a normal zinc level.

Antibiotics are frequently given. Ear infections are common, as are eczema, asthma, aching joints and bedwetting. Parents often report language difficulties and worry about developmental problems. There are many areas which need further urgent research involving nutrition, allergy, the immune and digestive systems and their impact on the health, behaviour and wellbeing of children.

We can provide information on the types of tests available and their cost (they are usually done by private clinics). We also have several publications including 'ADHD-Hyperactive Children, A Guide for Parents'. This covers the Feingold Food Programme and also has a wealth of other information related to diet and nutrition. Please refer to the final page of this book for further details of other related HACSG publications.

To close this short introduction on a personal note, I should like to give my warmest thanks to all those parents of hyperactive children who have made their contribution to this book, not only by virtue of the letters of support and encouragement written especially for this publication, but for their support and encouragement over the past three decades. I hope that those who read *The Proof of the Pudding* will appreciate something of the satisfaction we have felt over the years in being able to offer practical advice to parents. We are more than amply rewarded by the many success stories contained herein.

Sally Bunday, MBE
Founder & Secretary, HACSG

Photograph on facing page:
*Miles at eighteen months of age
with sister Mandy, eight, at the beach*

Better Children

A selection of letters from parents of ADHD/hyperactive children
whose health and behaviour have improved, sometimes quite dramatically,
after a change in their diets. The letters are a testimony to the fact that the
work of the HACSG has had a profound effect on many people's lives...

Miles, age eight

Paul

I feel our (your) greatest success has been with Paul. (Now there's one who was definitely headed towards a 'downward spiral' of EXPULS1ON>CAR THEFT> YOUNG OFFENDER >PRISON).

Paul has made a dramatic turnaround since taking his supplements ("Oh, by the way", he told me yesterday, "Miss, them tablet things haven't come yet !!"). I felt tears come into my eyes yesterday when I had a disruptive group, including Jamie whose Mum rang me up to make an appointment for a chat (referral to HACSG ?), only yesterday.

There were none of "your" pupils present in this "disruptive group", except Paul, who would normally be the worst pupil!

Instead, he was the politest pupil in the room, managing to control his reactions very sensibly. He has cut about 20 decibels off his loud voice, and he was able to speak to me quietly about how he would like to get good GCSE's in order to get into the Army when he leaves school. (He's bright and he could do it, even now).

I find it quite terrifying to think that a relatively inexpensive supply of supplements (less per annum than most people pay for their newspapers), is capable of transforming the life of a young person like Paul, so saving the Government tens of thousands of pounds in custody charges ! To say nothing of the cost of Case Conferences, as I've already mentioned to you.

I am writing to the Chairman of the School Governors, (a very caring chap), to put Paul's case to him, with details of his recent "transformation". It was him who stopped Paul being expelled three months ago. When I rang him at home and said I felt he needed to be referred to HACSG.

So, you have the satisfaction of knowing that one more young man will be prevented from joining the ranks of the future prison population. Personally I can't thank you enough.

I just wish more funds were available for the support of the tremendous work you are doing.

Sincerely,

Barbara

(Letter received June 19th, 1997)

Joe

Dear Mrs Bunday,
Just a quick up-date on my son, Joe.

After following the diet changes you sent us, and daily Zinc drops, Joe is a different child. In the past year we have moved house, changed schools and even been abroad on holiday - all things I thought would be impossible before, I truly cannot thank you enough.

Joe is now in Reception class at school and is doing brilliantly - the future Carol Vorderman maths genius is how teachers describe him!

After just a few weeks on the diet and drops, the change in him was noticeable and after a few months, the old Joe had gone and I had the gorgeous boy I always knew was inside him. The difference was truly staggering and even people who hardly knew him, noticed.
So thank you again for giving my boy a fair chance at childhood and for listening when no-one else would.

John

John's behavioural problems were so bad they nearly tore our family a part! Peter Brown and his wife, Mary, from Glasgow, have two children, John, 7 and Mark, 9. John suffered severe behavioural problems until August. Peter says that by the time John was three he had been excluded from two nurseries. He played too roughly, jumping on other children and running around screaming. Because he could lash out, he also found it very hard to make friends. We began to assume John had some kind of psychological problem.

Once he started school, we were given a report card each day saying that John had been running in the corridors, screaming and disobeying teachers. We were referred to family and educational psychologists. Eventually things got so bad that Mary and I decided to separate. The plan was for me to move with John to the remote Highlands where he could have a fresh start while Mary stayed in Glasgow with Mark.

While awaiting an appointment for John to be assessed for ADHD, Mary read an article about a child who had similar problems to John. He had been reformed when his parents removed E numbers from his diet.
Although John has always eaten lots of fresh fruit and vegetables, never a day went by when he didn't have sweets, crisps or fizzy drinks. But we cut

them from his diet and instead bought fruit chews and bars with no additives and preservatives, plain crisps and fresh fruit juices. And almost overnight John became a different boy. Calm, able to concentrate and more even-tempered. His teachers were astonished at the change. Within weeks John was voted Pupil Of The Week for good behaviour. I don't know who was more proud, him or us!

Lisa

Andrea from London is mum to Lisa, 7, and Clare, 2. Lisa seemed seriously disturbed until six months ago. Andrea says:

Lisa was two when she became a complete nightmare. Until then I'd prepared all her food from scratch and she'd been an angelic, peaceful child. Suddenly she would not do anything she was asked, threw tantrums over the slightest thing and was described as "the worst behaved child" in her nursery. She was also so hyperactive she couldn't sleep, I'd put her to bed at 8.30 pm and fight with her until midnight when she finally fell asleep exhausted. But by 2 am she'd be up again, wandering the house causing havoc.

One night she pulled the gas cooker on top of herself. Another time she ripped the door off the washing machine, then she flooded the bathroom and would regularly climb up on to the work-tops and empty the cupboards.

During the day Lisa was darting around and constantly hyper so I had to give up my job as a social worker to look after her. My mum used to help out, but eventually she said : "I'm frightened she'll get hurt". And a friend refused to take her any more when she ran into the road and a car had to swerve to avoid her. Shortly after Clare was born Lisa was referred to a child psychologist who wrongly suggested her problems were due to jealousy of the baby.

I got letters home from school every day saying Lisa had flooded the toilets or refused to sit down in class. And because she didn't know how to interact with other children, she had no friends. Things came to a head one night six months ago when we had a Chinese takeaway. Lisa had spare ribs in a deep red sauce and within minutes was screaming, kicking and lashing out. She then spent three hours crying. The following morning she had a rash on her face and my GP said it could have been an allergy to Monosodium Glutamate.

Desperate for answers, I did more research and came across the Hyperactive Children's Support Group. They advised me to remove all additives from Lisa's diet. Within three days she was sleeping through the night and she was so much calmer and happier, it was like getting back the baby she had once been.

The other day we were making popcorn and Lisa said, "Mummy, that's how my head used to feel, noisy like I had fizzy lemonade in it". So it's not difficult persuading her to cut out sweets and crisps because it lets her behave, and feel, like her old self!

Aaron

Aaron ran into the road during his tantrums!
Jane Williams and husband, Geoff, have two sons, Aaron, 11 , and David, 9. Aaron was often hyperactive and very argumentative until three years ago. Jane says : For years Aaron was a real Jekyll and Hyde character. Sometimes he was lovely and charming and other times angry and argumentative, and we had no idea what was responsible for these mood swings. He didn't know how to just play, he would take his toys apart and then climb on chairs or tables to get to ornaments which he would then drop and smash. Aaron woke at 5.30 am every day and from then on, was constantly on the go. As he got older his behaviour became more dangerous. On a couple of occasions he ran manically into the road and almost got run over. Cars had to screech to a halt to avoid him. It was as if his head was always somewhere else, preventing him from concentrating on what he was actually doing. At school the teachers would complain that, instead of working to the best of his ability, he would rush whatever he was doing just so he could be the first to finish. And at home he would cause arguments over the slightest thing. All I had to say was 'Aaron can you turn the TV over ?' or ' Will you go upstairs and get your jumper?' and he would get into a temper and start shouting.

I constantly asked myself "What am I doing wrong ?", worried it was down to poor parenting.

He also suffered from migraine, which I began to link to him eating certain foods. Then, three years ago, I started to realise Aaron's moods were also affected by things he ate. For instance, he would be in a terrible temper or really hyper soon after having snacks, sweets with artificial colourings, monosodium glutamate and sugar free dinks.

So I began to keep a record of everything Aaron ate and the effect it had on his mood. Seeing the link between the additives in these foods and his bad behaviour, I contacted the Hyperactive Children's Support Group. They sent me information about E numbers and the effect they can have on some children. So I cut them out of Aaron's diet and the change in him was incredible. He was so much more relaxed, no longer hyper and he slept until a reasonable hour each day.

His concentration, both at home and at school, is so much improved and he is a real pleasure to be around. It is frightening to realise that E numbers had seriously affected my son's personality!

Mick & MSG, et al

Another of those shocking migraine headaches which are unbearable and play heck with trying to get anything done. Suddenly Rosemary said, "Here - wonder if it's that Chinese meal that we had the other evening?"

I looked at her with my slightly blurred vision and asked, "Chinese meal, what's that got to do with migraine?"

Rosemary was a biology teacher and well into such things. She fired back at me, 'Well, it has MSG in it. And I've heard that it can cause problems.' "What's MSG?", I asked, never having heard of it.

I got the usual impatient shrug by return but she went on, 'It stands for monosodium glutamate, it's a flavour enhancer and helps to make food taste good!'

"Oh," I said. "It makes food taste good but gives you a headache. Can that be right?"

"Well, it doesn't affect everybody, and it doesn't affect you all the time, does it!"

I guess she was right. I didn't suffer all the time but could see that continual use could cause it to build up until it reached a point that it had a disastrous side effect. And that side effect takes some living with -ask anyone who suffers from headaches! Just to think, I had suffered from migraine headaches all my life and all I needed to do was to stop eating things with MSG in! Well, not quite.

It took a while for the dizziness and blurred vision to wear off and when it did we were able to sit down and discuss the problem rationally.

Rosemary had recently heard of a newly published book called 'E for Additives' and we went out and bought a copy - the revelations were amazing and just browsing through it we were shocked to see the many questionable additives that were included in our daily diet and the consequences they had on some people. But not everybody, some were more prone to effects than others. Some were reckoned to be all right for adults but not for babies!

One thing led to another and before long - and after reading through the book carefully - came to the conclusion that the subject needed more study on my part.

By sheer coincidence I heard of an organisation called the Hyperactive Children's Support Group that had recently been formed to help parents of hyperactive children to overcome the problems that they were having. (This was back in the 1980's.) I joined the HACSG and it was one of the best things that I ever did, it also gave me a greater understanding of the children that I was teaching in my secondary school.

Following advice in their book 'Hyperactive Child' I allowed Rosemary to impose an 'Elimination Diet' on me and for a whole year I ate and drank only things that we knew to be free from harmful additives; I also stopped cheese, chocolate and coffee and a few more items that we had been advised to be wary of.

The result was very surprising and I suffered no more migraine attacks and - what was even more surprising - I slowed down and became far less hyperactive. Hyperactive ? I never realised that I was but indeed there was a marked difference in my behaviour.

After a year Rosemary considered that she could re-introduce suspect foods to try and find out which ones affected me. Surprisingly, I could eat and drink most things but we were able to pinpoint a lot of questionable additives. We already knew about MSG but a preservative used in meats (Sodium nitrate) had an even worse effect and, when allowed to build up in my system caused severe hyperactivity, convulsions and dizziness. As a result I eliminated corned beef, bacon and similar processed meats from my diet.

I was now becoming sufficiently well informed on the subject and I took it into my own hands to advise the parents of children who I was teaching about harmful additives and gave them print-outs and copies of the HACSG newsletter to guide them. I even gave information to the local press who kindly published an article on the subject for me. Unbelievably the newspaper article elicited a haughty response from a manufacturer of additives who heavily defended the right to produce and distribute them, claiming at the same time that they were completely harmless.

Amongst the familiar additives that we should beware of are preservatives, sweeteners, flavour enhancers and colourings. I personally never buy anything from a supermarket without first diligently reading the label. And I avoid anything in a restaurant that appears dubious. People who are dyslexic (I suffer from dyscalculia which is a similar problem but concerns numeracy) are more prone to allergies it seems than the average person and, as a dyslexia teacher, I have come to accept that the average dyslexic pupil will possibly suffer from food allergies and, sadly, ADHD (Attention Deficit Hyperactivity Disorder).

It is not always doubtful additives that affect the child either; in many cases it may be a hypersensitive reaction to things like milk (lactose), wheat (gluten), citric acid and sometimes eggs. As before, the way forward is to use an elimination diet to find out which are the culprits. Keeping a daily diary of the food that they eat is very helpful too and makes an excellent reference work.

Artificial sweeteners and colourings are good examples of what should be avoided whenever possible - they are there primarily to attract children but can produce very harmful effects.

What of some of these questionable additives, where do they come from and what are they made of? Colouring may be made from Azo or Coal tar dyes and Sunset Yellow (E110) is one that was in the limelight a short time ago. It has been suggested that it may contain traces of 'Sudan 1' which recently triggered a panic in the food marketing world. Like various other additives it is actually banned in some European countries. And one would think that with all the adverse publicity these additives have that the chemical industry would take heed - not a bit of it; medicines, toothpastes, mouthwashes etc. all have their fair share of additives and letters to the manufactures only elicit replies that the additives have been fully tested and have no harmful effects!

Unfortunately, 'E for Additives' is out of print but you may be able to obtain a copy from your local library.

Miles and Lucy

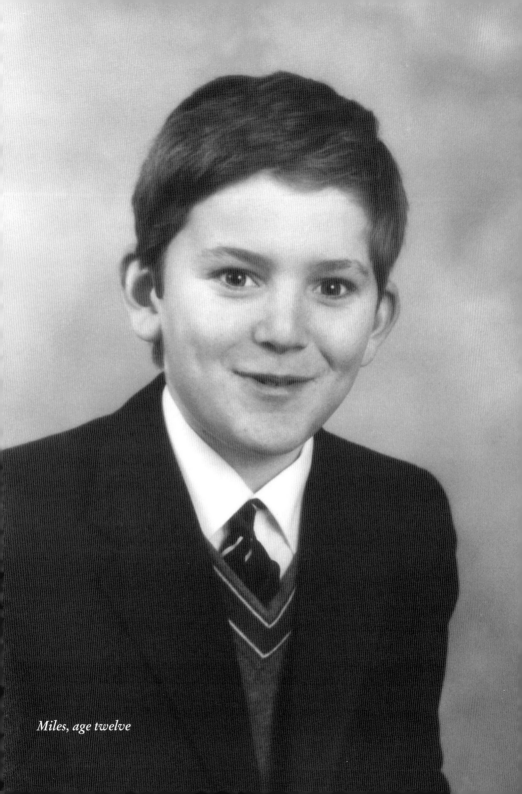

Miles, age twelve

The New Class

You walk into the classroom and gaze down at the array of expectant smiling faces - looking at you, weighing you up. It's a bit uneven isn't it, there are over thirty of them and only one of you. There will be over thirty different conceptions of you and probably all will be different; some will think, 'Oh, he looks a hard case, better buckle down and do what he says.' A few more will be thinking, ' He's a pushover, we can play him up and get away with it.' Others, 'I hope he's interested in sport, aeroplanes, pet rabbits, word games and so on.'

You're lucky, you've done it hundreds of times - it's called experience. The first time, all those years ago, was quite difficult but it got easier as you went along; you can't buy experience; you have to work for it. Looking down at all those faces 40 years ago was quite daunting and you were probably more scared of them than they were of you. But now it's different! You've got plenty of time to study the faces and personalities.

Maintaining that quiet scrutiny is also imposing your will on them - the longer you continue to study them quietly the longer they will feel obliged to do the same. There will be all types in the class and you know from experience and statistics that three or four will be dyslexic (mostly boys on a ratio of four to one); they will not be a problem if they get specialised attention and lots of reassurance, they will be of above average intelligence - good at sport and very creative but will have the greatest difficulty expressing themselves in writing. Give them as much one to one help as possible; teach them to listen and apply spelling rules and assign lots of praise. If the condition is severe, make sure that the parents and staff are aware of it and arrange an interview with the educational psychologist for a full educational assessment.

If you are lucky there will be a broad band of average, well behaved, hard working children in the middle of the group. They are a bonus; you tell them what to do and they do it; you tell them to be quiet and they quieten down; you seek their co-operation and they co-operate. Wonderful!

But what's this - a few at the back of the class are beginning to get restless. You had noticed anyway that they were paying less than full attention to you and now they are getting really fidgety. One seems to be worse than the rest and even as you watch he clumsily takes a sticky looking sweet from his pocket and slips it noisily into his mouth. You don't need to say anything, just point at him and then at the waste bin in the corner. If you have assumed the right expression he will obediently walk over and drop the offending morsel into the bin. As he passes you on the way back you hold out your hand for him to reluctantly hand over his goodies. One look is enough, the sweets are from a well known manufacturer but one glance at the label tells you that they are full of undesirable additives - colours, flavourings and sweeteners. You are well aware of the likelihood of food additives causing hyperactivity and lack of concentration and here in your new class are some prime examples. You are fully aware of the devastating effect that a few additives have on you - monosodium glutamate, tartrazine and sodium nitrate - all of which were responsible for you getting interested in the subject in the first place. You look down at the fidgety offenders and wonder how much their parents know about food allergies and the disastrous reactions that junk foods can inflict upon their children..........

ADHD or Attention Deficit Hyperactive Disorder is becoming more common and increasingly more devastating as manufacturers continue to incorporate a wide range of dubious chemicals into their products. Some Headmasters have cracked down on what is sold in school tuck shops and many parents have got the message and imposed restrictions upon their child's diet. Some parents have carried out joint programmes with their children's schools to eliminate doubtful additives from their diets with outstanding results - improved learning, better concentration, elimination of behavioural problems and better all round performance!

That's right, when dealing with growing children certainly, 'Ignore bad behaviour and praise good behaviour'! But can you afford to ignore the causes? Dyslexic children are more likely to suffer allergies than the average child and the allergy may well give rise to behavioural problems and seemingly uncontrollable reactions which are frequently termed ADHD or Attention Deficit Hyperactivity Disorder. Diet plays a big part in the problem and there is an almost endless list of doubtful foods and additives that may give rise to your child's behaviour difficulties. But let's have a look at some of the symptoms; he may well be very disruptive and noisy, always on the go and often aggressive. He may have sleep problems and be awake most of the night. His behaviour may be very erratic and he may go to great lengths to gain attention, even to the point of attacking you in public. He is probably a 'nightmare' to teaching staff at school and very severely lacking in concentration.

Some children have a natural intolerance to cow's milk, oranges (citric acid) and wheat which can be fairly easily eliminated from their diet. But it is the endless of list of junk food, flavourings, preservatives, colourings, artificial sweeteners and doubtful additives that are difficult to track down and control.

If your child suffers allergic reactions then watch carefully for when these are most severe and then look back to see if there is anything that he has consumed a short time ago that may have caused them. It can be very helpful to keep a strict diary of his daily intake of food; definitely inform the school canteen of any food that he must avoid and try to gain the cooperation of the school tuck shop too. If he is being entertained at a party at a friend's home make sure that the host is informed - it may be thought that, 'Oh, this is a special day, a little bit of this or that won't do him any harm.' Make no mistake about it - it will!

The transformation that can take place when an offending food or additive is removed from his diet has to be seen to be believed; it will take a lot of dedication on the part of both the parent and the child to reach this point - perhaps the most difficult goal is to win the cooperation of the child. Basically you should avoid junk food and anything that is steeped in a mass of chemical preservatives, colourings and flavourings. Become a dedicated reader of the list of 'Ingredients' on packaged food and drink when shopping at a supermarket, avoid any that are doubtful. Medicinal items such as tablets, toothpaste and dental mouthwash may be hazardous as some contain colourings like Tartrazine E102 which is actually banned in some countries! A recent finding was that Calcium Propionate E282 which is added to bread to extend its life when wrapped in plastic bags can also produce undesirable reactions.

Is there a cure for Hyperactivity? Well, the best advice is to remove the cause as suggested above. There are many recorded cases where an understanding Headmaster has advised the school tuck-shop on what they can safely sell to pupils, the result has been a measurable decline in hyperactivity and bad behaviour and a very pleasing rise in concentration and examination results.

Fish oils and Evening Primrose Oil are known to improve concentration and general performance in addition to reducing hyperactivity. In general it is wise to include a good proportion of Essential Fatty Acids (EFA's) known technically as Omega-3 and Omega-6 in your child's diet and these will be present in oily fish but remember at all times consult your doctor or a qualified dietician.

Mick Ford

Dear Sally...

I'm writing to share our experience of an improved diet, as well as other possibilities that could contribute towards better behaviour and happier children!

We have usually had what we considered a fairly healthy diet, but noticed a gradual decline in our son's behaviour and happiness which we later realised was related to the amount of sugar that he was eating.

It began with his strong desire for sugary drinks, like squash, and reached a very difficult peak when we had to leave a rented house, due to its being sold. We went to live with relatives and our diet began to include new things which were, unbeknown to us, creating more of the same trouble !

A simple snack, such as a slice of bread and jam, would, quite literally, transform our intellectual and reflective son into a raging monster ! The effect would last a whole afternoon, for example, and include things like : punching, kicking, screaming and biting, as well as throwing chairs. Any attempt at putting him in another room would fail and the only action we could take was to either pin him down until the tantrum stopped or put him in the garden (where he would throw other things). He would constantly ring the doorbell and scream at us to let him back in immediately. The whole family was utterly depressed, including our son, as he spent the day feeling angry and frustrated.

We talked about what might be causing the trouble. Stress due to moving house, worries, etc., but came to the conclusion that, although our children are relatively boisterous, an increase in sugar consumption had made a huge difference to both of them. Our daughter was less likely to notice danger or other' feelings, as well as having difficulty in sitting still.

We noticed a huge difference when sugar was cut out and also took the children for a non-invasive allergy test with a nutritionist/allergy tester. It cost £25 each and involved their holding a bar connected to an electronic machine, which measured the body's electrical responses to a wide range of foods. When a vial of each food was held, a higher sound was produced if the body could tolerate it. A lower one if not (as far as I can remember). Doing this we could then be aware of other allergies, (wheat, soya, sugar and even sweetcorn for my daughter). Since then, things have improved even more and we have discovered many alternatives to the 'banned' foods. (Junk food and chemical additives are well avoided too, of course). Health food shops have been particularly productive and helpful. (I also carry an additive booklet on shopping trips).

Aside from diet, encouragement and understanding have had amazing effects and we do use some small reward systems too. Visible consequences seem very beneficial.

I hope this has been helpful to anyone who might read it and good luck to everyone in their family life.

The B. Family

Michael

I feel compelled to write to you, as with your help I have now got an adorable 4 year old boy, whom I now love very much. Not the case, just six months ago. He has gone from being an aggressive, spiteful child with more tantrums in a day than I care to remember, to a very loving, affectionate, bright and intelligent boy -all because of his diet.

Following the advice given in the booklet, we have eliminated the 'culprits' from the diet, mainly 'colours', chocolate and orange and many preservatives.

We have occasional 'blips' as we call them, but these are usually caused by M having foodstuffs that he shouldn't have, through no fault of his own. He now knows what he can and can't have and willingly goes without.

If only I had asked for your help earlier, I could have avoided the hate and the unrest in the family. I had to have a course of antidepressants and finally give up my job as a midwife. Life suddenly looks very rosy.

I hope you continue your good work and I willingly give my name, address and telephone number as a point of contact should anyone need my help or support. If only people would recognise that this is a major problem and hyperactive children can really be helped.

With many thanks,

Mrs A. G.

Daniel

I would like to say a very big 'thank-you' for the information you kindly sent me and for your advice on the telephone. I have read through all of the literature, visited libraries, my GP, Daniel's migraine clinic and the GNC Health store and have put Daniel on an eating plan similar to the Feingold diet. Just cutting out additives, artificial preservatives and the deadly artificial sweeteners has made an enormous difference in Daniel's behaviour. Many thanks again for your support and help and I will keep you posted on Daniel's progress.

Best regards,

Sonya (Name & address supplied)

James

After cutting out colours from my son's diet his behaviour has improved dramatically (although he was not hyperactive) I am therefore looking for further information on E-numbers; whether you had details of foods they are present in and perhaps which supermarkets. Annatto seems to produce the more violent behaviour and is regarded as natural I believe!

Thank you very much,

Yours sincerely,

Diana (Name & address supplied)

Connor

We have already seen a difference in Connor (9.1.99) since cutting out additives and colours. We are eager to try the Feingold Diet and have bought Efalex which Connor has just started taking.

Yours gratefully,

Joan (Name & address supplied)

Nick

Nick is progressing very well! He is taking B6, Zinc & EPO and his 'outbursts' are getting fewer & fewer thank God ! He also looks better, his eyes are more normal.

Many thanks and regards,

Jackie (Name & address supplied)

Thomas

My son, Thomas, has not been 'diagnosed' with anything (apart from our GP saying he is 'hyper-intelligent') but I have been following the Feingold Diet from about 18 months ago when I first found it on your website. He has always been a difficult child and I have found the information your group provides to be invaluable.

Tom will be five next month. We have been going through the 'terrible two's' for about four years now. I really notice a difference when he has 'forbidden' foods and find that a diet consisting of pineapple juice, organic everything, cheese sandwiches, plain crisps and no preservatives, colourings or flavourings seems to really work. When Tom has a 'funny turn' his eyes glaze over, he seems incoherent and indifferent to what is going on around him.

Jumping around etc., etc! My Health Visitor comes to me for dietary advice for difficult children. Shouldn't it be the other way round? Keep up the good work!

Regards,

Brenda (Name & address supplied)

David

Just watched the programme tonight about the Jackson family which moved me to remember the past. I contacted you 16 years ago at my wit's end with my youngest son. Your support was second to none and got us on the road to finding solutions to D 's behaviour problems.

David has not had any problems whatsoever since he was 5. By 7 even his coordination problems were gone. He has no food-sensitivities; nothing left from such a difficult beginning. He is a delightful, lovely and wonderful 18 year-old who has just taken four A levels and is waiting calmly for his results. I am so proud of him ! His behaviour reports from school have been second to none and he is well-liked in our community for his kindness and compassionate care for others.

We have worked our socks off and spent a fortune to sort him out and it was worth every effort. However, we could not have got there without people like you ! You and your mother spent hours on the phone to me at a time when we were completely isolated from life.

How can I ever thank you enough. On behalf of myself and my son I thank you from the bottom of my heart!

With warmest regards,

Carol (Name and address supplied)

Sarah and Nicole

Thank you for your resource pack regarding hyperactivity in children. It has helped me no end with my two daughters who both react to additives. It is so surprising to find so many artificial colourings and preservatives in today's foods.

I now check everything when I do my weekly shopping for such additives and I take the list with me to check. I have seen such an improvement within my two daughters behaviour ever since I have used your list for additives within food.

Thank you for your help and support with this matter.

Mother (Name & address supplied)

Mike

Our son Mike has always been a difficult child. A poor sleeper, irritable, 'crier', generally unco-operative. As he got older he became aggressive and angry. We heard about your diet scheme and decided to try it. We felt we had nothing to lose !

The results have been dramatic. The first 3 weeks we saw many withdrawal symptoms. More anger, more tantrums and incredible tiredness. Mike slept for 14 hours a night! having never had an uninterrupted night in four years.

We now manage the diet fairly easily with occasional 'blips' at Christmas and birthday parties. Mike is calmer, happy, less aggressive and more loving. He is coping with Nursery and we are positive about his entry into school in September.

Patrick

We have been following your dietary advice for our son since November 2001. The diet has been a great success in alleviating our son's behaviour problem. We are so pleased with your support we would like to become members of the group. I am willing to provide a local ear for new people thinking of trying the diet if you feel this would be of benefit to anyone. Yours sincerely, (Name & address supplied)

Jamie

Whilst recently visiting my daughter in the United States we 'discovered' the Feingold Association which she then joined, resulting in dramatically improved health, behaviour and sleep-patterns for one of her children and this in a family which had previously considered that it ate healthily to begin with!

The Feingold pack included a book listing brand-names and supermarket brands of every category of food, toiletries etc. which were free of artificial colour and of the most common chemical allergens. Do you have such a book of British brands as part of your available information?

I feel so strongly about the incredible change in one little boy resulting from cutting out certain every-day foods, or from switching brand-names that my second question is whether you have any objection to my writing a letter to a national newspaper and giving your website address as a contact?

I look forward to hearing from you.
Yours faithfully, (Name & address supplied)

Carl

We have just started the Feingold Diet with my 14 year old son, plus all the vitamins and oils. After one week we have a 'new' boy - my husband said today that he can talk to him for the first time in two years. He was so aggressive at home and disruptive at school; one crisis after another and no family life. We ended up in family therapy where the psychiatrist diagnosed ADHD and wanted to try medication.

Thank God for the Feingold Diet and help like yours!

Many thanks,

Aileen (Name & address supplied)

Sam

I just wanted to let you know, some years ago now you helped me with my son who is salicylate sensitive. He has just been offered a place at Cambridge University and it's all thanks to you! Without your help schooling would have been a complete disaster and I dread to think what would have become of him.

You saved our lives and our sanity and have given him such a tremendous future -*THANK YOU*.

With my very best wishes,

T . (Name & address supplied)

Daniel

When Daniel was first born I knew there was something different about him. He was so advanced as a baby. Didn't crawl, got up and walked at 9 months, then he became a mini-tornado, destroying anything in his path. I started to avoid visiting relatives and friends and became quite isolated. I started to see a connection between certain foods and Daniel's behaviour, but when I ask doctors they dismissed the connection.

Two years passed by when Daniel is admitted to hospital with stomach pains and doctors notice he is very hyperactive, but still dismissed his diet. On release from hospital I went to the Library and found the book by Sally Bunday and Co., called "The Hyperactive Child'. I was amazed by what I was reading and immediately changed Daniel's diet. His behaviour improved by 50%. He could concentrate for longer and became a much calmer child. Daniel was diagnosed with ADHD while in hospital. I believe through changing Daniel's diet and finding the Hyperactive Children's Support Group, it changed my son's life. I didn't medicate my son. The diet and advice from Sally Bunday did that for my son Daniel.

Sally and her mother's work over 30 years did not get enough recognition and I wrote to Buckingham Palace to recognise the wonderful ladies who have spent most of their lives helping our children.

Thank you Sally and your late Mother, Irene Colquhoun, for changing my son's life forever.

Teresa Fitzgerald, Liverpool.

George

Back in the seventies my father Mick Ford, discovered that his awful migraines were caused by food intolerances. He did an elimination diet and avoided colourings, flavourings, preservatives, MSG, chocolate, nuts, cheese and nitrates for a whole year and was fine. He then went back and found that MSG and Nitrates were clearly the most definite causes.

Dad then became involved with the HACSG and is still involved thirty years later.

I was a child then, and learnt my lessons well about food. I trained as a homoeopath and studied nutritional biochemistry along the way.

When I had my own children I knew that the chances of them being sensitive were very likely so I have always avoided unsuitable foods. My older son is now nearly six and he has always been a lively character. He cannot concentrate for more than a second on written work. He takes Veg EPA, the oil containing evening primrose oil and fish oil without DHA, twice the recommended dose of multi-nutrients, and a homoeopathic remedy. I think he is the type of person who would have been badly affected by junk foods; he reacts to sugar quite badly.

I have been quite worried about him and recently had him tested for scoptopic sensitivity syndrome (Irlen Syndrome), and he was prescribed a coloured overlay. To my amazement the next time he tried to read, he read the whole book by himself and concentrated perfectly well. We are off to get him some coloured glasses for him in a week's time. His attention span is markedly different now when reading with the overlay. His concentration problem it seems is only partly due to foods - we shall see. I expect it will take him a while to adjust to the lenses. His school want me to have him assessed by a paediatric specialist but I am hoping this will not be necessary.

In essence, we need to be barking up the right tree to solve these problems and information of the sort that we get from your organisation is the key. I want to thank the HACSG for their wonderful integrity, energy and support.

Sue Cook

Sean

Sean has always been a very active child with an insatiable curiosity, a high degree of sensitivity and a fair amount of wanting to be the one in charge! He can be impulsive, determined and imaginative. We have to be vigilant as there is always the "X Factor". You just never know what idea he will suddenly decide to act upon! As a baby, Sean needed to be kept constantly occupied and slept little during the day. Being big for his age, he needed copious volumes of milk and food. His growth rate seemed to frequently make him very tired and emotional, but it was when he was around two and a half that he began to have mood swings. After eating certain foods or drinking certain things, he would, within half an hour or so, change from being happy, smiling and kind to being volatile and angry.

I remember one day he ate some sweets which were brightly coloured, almost luminous. A short time later he was sweeping ornaments off shelves, trying to pull curtains down and crying. When 1 tried to calm him down and tell him that this was not allowed, he flew into such a rage that he actually pulled the fridge out from under the worktop ! My attempts to regain calm and control resulted in a major tantrum and he ran into another room, throwing himself on the floor. Sweaty and exhausted, he cried. All I could do was cuddle him until he was calm and then explain that he must not throw ornaments, etc.!

We had repeated incidents like this. On the worst occasions he would even scratch and bite. Discipline was difficult as he was obviously distressed and frightened by his own reactions. It was a behaviour that seemed totally out of his control. It was also difficult as we couldn't let him think it was acceptable to behave like that We developed a strategy of regaining calmness and then talking to him and enforcing the idea that such and such was not allowed and why it wasn't.

Sean has always been brilliant at going to bed and sleeping almost immediately, exhausted by all that activity and growing. However, on days when he had an "episode", he would frequently have hallucinatory nightmares, so scary that he would be frightened to get back into bed and would want to sleep on the floor on the other side of the room. We had to use reward stickers for a while to get him into bed without upset!

At Nursery, Sean was doing very well. He was loved by all the staff and with his excellent memory, was learning easily. However, we had certain days when we would be told "I don't know what was wrong with him today, but..." The Nursery Staff were fantastic. In particular the lady in charge, Adrienne. We had frequent discussions about how Sean could "change", often after a meal or a holiday when he ate more ice-cream, drank more squash and ate at different restaurants.

I had begun to look at Sean's diet at home and switched from squash, for which he always had a raging thirst, to watered down apple juice. Within a few days, Sean was less volatile, was no longer in constant motion, his night time sleep improved and the nightmares vanished. I researched more and more and bought a book, "E for Additives" by Maurice Hanssen. The HACSG have contributed to this book and provided a list of additives to be avoided, giving both their chemical name and E number. I began to remove the listed additives from Sean's diet and at the same time, some fruits which contain Salicylates, also implicated in fuelling hyperactivity. I contacted the HACSG and enrolled as a member.

The change in Sean was remarkable. We had far less incidents in which he seemed possessed! He was generally calmer, able to sit still for longer and able to concentrate better. As time has gone by, we have re-introduced some things into Sean's diet and if there is an adverse effect, removed them again until gradually we think we have it just about right. For Sean certain things have a pronounced effect and we avoid them at all costs. For instance. Sodium Benzoate or E211, which is a preservative found in drinks, notably for Sean, squash. It is also found in handwashes which can also dramatically affect Sean, whether it is because he sucked his thumb or if it is absorbed through the skin., we do not know. Last time he was in contact with it, he had such a 'turn' that I ended up crunching my car on the drive wall in my anxiety to get us both into the house!

In addition to eliminating things from Sean's diet, I have also introduced supplements as recommended by the HACSG. Many hyperactive children, particularly boys, lack Zinc and for various reasons, are unable to metabolise Essential Fatty Acids which are found in the oils of seafood and certain plants. Together with daily Zinc drops and EyeQ liquid containing fish oils and Evening Primrose Oil, Sean's insatiable thirst has vanished His eczema/dry skin condition has improved and his tiredness is not so overpowering. I also notice that Sean is less clumsy and doesn't fall over quite as often and finds it much easier to catch a ball. All these things changed within a couple of weeks.

As a family, we are constantly learning more and more about additives, whether they are colours, preservatives or flavourings. We follow quite closely the guidelines of the Feingold Diet which is recommended by the HACSG and have tweaked it to make Sean's diet as varied as possible. For instance, whilst Sean can eat cherry tomatoes, plum tomatoes or tomatoes on the vine can cause him to bite, scratch or pinch. Blackcurrant in any form is a disaster for us and we have to revert to psychological tactics to maintain the family sanity. Sean is a wonderful, happy boy who is loving, clever, kind to pets and loves school. He has some great friends and lives an exciting and stable life.

His ex-nursery hold Sean up as an example to parents of new children and include a mention of additives, etc., in their induction talk. Both the nursery and us have been able to help several parents who have experienced the same problems.

We cannot thank the HACSG enough, particularly Sally Bunday, whose kindness and pioneering spirit are an example to us all. Hopefully one day these substances will be removed from foods altogether. Many companies are beginning to change without government legislation and the enforcement of the Foods Standards Agency. Sometimes scientific facts are 'overlooked' in world economics and we may only hope that one day parents will not have to do months of research in order to protect the health of their children. Unlike Sean, some children and their parents will never discover the 'secret'. It is up to us to help them.

Pam Milne, January 2007.

Robin

We noticed a difference in our third child, a son, when he was two and thought he was gifted. He learnt things quickly, was on the go all the time, and was extremely inquisitive. He was excluded from school soon after he started as he lashed out at a teacher. The headteacher's comment was that they had never seen another child like him; 'on a one to one basis he lights up, but in a class full of children he is a nightmare'.

He was diagnosed with ADHD and Asperger Syndrome just before the age of seven. I think I contacted Sally prior to the exclusion, tried fishoils and at one time cut out everything that looked like or was an additive. We had to take the medication route just to keep in school. Children like my son live in their own world and it is the parents that give them everything they need but are isolated in doing so. Sally has been a vital source of support over the telephone for me, and many parents like me. For a school to tap into these children they have to go the extra mile and put up with a lot of blips, but I found one of these for my son eventually. Robin is now fifteen, and he is in the Air Cadets and has passed some GCSE's early and has a huge potential.

I thank Sally for the support and for all the literature she has provided over the years and I hope the HACSG in its 30th year has many years of success ahead of it.

Norma

Some words from Tom

At the moment I live a roughly 'normal' life (even though I try and avoid the norm in most instances!) and I often wonder what would have become of me if it weren't for all the help and support from my Mum and in turn the help and support the HACSG gave to my Mum.

My attention still wanders from time to time, and I go through mood swings (who doesn't?) but without the help from my Mum and the HACSG and the diet which I'm on I don't think I'd be able to cope in the job I'm in or be able to interact with all the friends I currently have. In short I wouldn't be able to live like I do now. When (occasionally) I stray from my diet I can feel all the problems coming back and it's only through the continual and on-going support from my Mum and my family that I can carry on with leading a fun and active life (Will - squash rematch whenever you fancy it!!).

Now that my Mum has a little more spare time (and Will and I have moved out of home) she continues to help other families and other children and I see many of them share the problems which Will and I faced and it's great that the HACSG exists so that my Mum can pass on her wisdom, knowledge, friendship and support to all the other families and children who need help.

Without the HACSG and without my Mum who knows where I'd be.

Thank you from me and thank you from all the other kids and families you've helped…

Duncan

My son, Duncan, was about 18 months old when he started being disruptive in social situations and having terrible tantrums. He hit other children, pushed them to the ground grabbed everything within reach causing havoc and destruction wherever he went. He always had a smile on his face and no matter that he was disciplined or removed from the situation all the time, he just didn't seem able to stop himself.

Taking him to playgroups, parties and playgrounds became a nightmare. My heart kept breaking as other mothers looked on disapprovingly and removed their children. He stopped being invited anywhere and when he was, he invariably hurt another child or damaged something.

Duncan couldn't sit still or concentrate on any activity and I felt increasingly stressed and exhausted.

One day I had taken Duncan to a ball pit area when he proceeded to thump two children in two minutes, I dragged him away and was about to take him home when one of the dad's approached me. I braced myself for an onslaught of what a bad mother I was when he said, ' my son was like yours, but I changed his diet, removing additives and colourings and he has calmed down. You might like to contact the Hyperactive Children's Support Group.'

I thanked him and left feeling intrigued but not really believing it. I told my husband and parents about it and they said try it, what have you got to lose? I admit I bristled a bit thinking it was a criticism of what I was feeding him, but then I started to look at food labels I was taken aback. The children's yoghurts he ate were full of colourings and flavourings as were the squash, soft drinks, etc. I had no idea and I felt terrible.

I phoned HACSG who were brilliant and when I received the literature, I started his new diet. I was dreading it as Duncan had become fussy with his food and would have terrible tantrums if denied chocolate or coke. However, I was startled. Within two days he was calmer. Everyone noticed enough to remark on it. I looked at food labels all the time and found additives in almost everything attractively packaged for children. I felt angry as I felt my son and I had lost a year of our life. We have carried on with the diet and found the change remarkable. Duncan seems to be able to listen now, whereas before, it had never seemed to register.

Duncan continues to take vitamin and fish supplements which seem to really help him and if he has a cake or fizzy drinks now, he is not very affected as I believe his system is clear of these additives.

Duncan is 13 now and he has passed entrance exams, is studying well and is the school football captain and a County tennis player. I don't believe he would have achieved any of these without following the advice of the HACSG. I always loved my son, and am now also very proud of him. Thank you for giving him his life back.

Stella,
December 2006

Stephen

Looking back on a childhood with food and chemical allergies.

My son, Stephen, was born in 1972 and thankfully now enjoys good health but looking back through my records of the first ten years of his life is a stark reminder of the problems he had with severe food and chemical allergies. His symptoms started with hyperactivity and then eczema but as he became more chemically sensitive went on to include gastric upsets, migraine, dizzy and fainting fits and finally seizures. At his worst point he was reacting to milk, cheese, beef, all grains except rice, all legumes, eggs, pork, potatoes, tomatoes and tap water. His inhalant allergies included petrol and diesel fumes, plastics, natural gas, printing ink, wool and house dust mites. I realise that he was a very extreme case, approaching what was known as 'Total Allergy Syndrome', but I thought it might be of interest to hear something of his story and, perhaps, give some encouragement and hope to other parents in a similar situation.

Stephen had a normal birth, if with a rather long labour. I was, however, very disappointed when I was unable to establish breast feeding at all. He was a big baby and was always hungry and so I introduced mixed feeding much earlier than is advised today. By the age of six months he was already hyperactive, being very difficult to hold or comfort and also had sleeping problems. By the age of three he had become very difficult to control, with frequent temper tantrums and was having repeated chest and ear infections requiring antibiotics.

When he was six, I read of the HACSG and on Sally's advice started him on an additive free and whole food diet. Within one week he was sleeping right through the night and his appetite and behaviour improved. He had been very difficult about his food, only eating the usual convenience foods and hardly sitting still long enough to eat a proper meal. For the next three years he followed the pattern of being reasonably well all summer when he could be out in the open air, with a return of his symptoms each autumn, getting progressively worse each winter. He would come down with a bad infection each February, starting with chicken pox when he was seven and then influenza and tonsillitis in subsequent years and after each his allergic symptoms were more severe. In March 1980, his catarrh and chest infections had got very much worse and we began to wonder if food allergies could be the cause. We tried taking him off milk and cheese and were pleased when his symptoms cleared. By March 1981 he was very much worse again, now having sickness, diarrhoea and migraine as well as his other symptoms. We tried him on a gluten free diet and again he picked up. By March 1982 he had become worse still and was reacting to a whole host of foods with some extreme reactions.

We had exhausted the National Health facilities in our area and were put in touch with some clinical ecologists. He was put on a rotated diet to help his food tolerances and had skin tests done for chemical allergies. This was helpful as it confirmed that he reacted to all the chemicals tested, but was a disaster as he was made very much worse as a result of the testing and was not helped by the drops supplied. We then went to great lengths to clear our house of everything he was reacting to, including having the gas fire and cooker removed, taking up the foam backed carpets and removing as much plastic as possible. In desperation we turned to a homeopath to try to find a way out. Homeopathy was something we knew nothing about at the time, but for Stephen it worked wonders. Over the next eighteen months

Stephen had many constitutional remedies prescribed and also homeopathic doses of all his chemical allergens as shown in the tests. The improvement was quite dramatic when he was given homeopathic petroleum followed by plastic, natural gas, house dust mite etc, etc. On Sally's advice again, Stephen had been on vitamin and mineral supplements with evening primrose oil for some time, but the homeopath put him on courses of very high vitamin doses with great effect.

Looking back through all this now I realise how much we learnt along the way and how differently and how much sooner we would have tackled things if we could have the time over again. One good thing to have come of it all was that I went on to train as a kinesiologist with particular interest in allergies. When considering possible causes of Stephen's chemical allergies, it is perhaps significant that I worked as a laboratory technician for eight years before he was bom, handling formaldehyde as well as solvents and other chemicals. Also, in his early years we did not have central heating and relied on a gas fire as well as having a gas cooker. Then when he was three we had the loft sprayed for woodworm. We used a local firm and were not given any warnings about keeping out of the rooms afterwards. Stephen had an attic bedroom with three hatches into the roof space. The clear message from all this must be to reduce contact with chemicals as far as possible, eat whole food and preferably organic diet and to consider complementary therapies.

We are very grateful to Sally for starting us on the road to recovery for Stephen and for her gentle and sensible support over the years.

Nutrition & behaviour - our story

Early History

H. was a (breast fed) colicky baby who suffered from reflux and would cry day and night. We were told that he would grow out of it, with the unspoken implication that at 35 I was an older career mother struggling to adjust to motherhood! After five months of hell and a chance comment by a friend, we finally identified that H was Lactose Intolerant. Switching to a Lactose Free cow's formula was like a miracle, we finally saw the true baby smiling through and not in pain. However, H seemed to be constantly ill although he never really got a temperature. He suffered from colds and constant ear infections and glue ear for which he was prescribed antibiotics several times before he was even 1 year old. We eventually switched to a Soya formula at about eight months old and within 24 hours H. had his first "real" temperature which went so high that he had convulsions, it was as if his immune system had finally started working, so H had no dairy products for the next four years.

Little did we realise the damage that these early problems had done to H's bowel, although thanks to the wonders of the WWW I had the foresight to delay the introduction of Gluten until about 15 months and (after much research of my own) we requested mercury-free initial DTP vaccinations" and decided that not only was the MMR far too risky but the single measles vaccination was also dangerous for a child with bowel problems, a decision we have never regretted.

Behavioural Issues

H was always considered a "challenging" child, but we were told he was just a very bright child that needed lots of stimulation. Being our first child we thought that it was just the "terrible two's" although it started at 12 months old and got worse as he got older. Some of the behavioural traits are seen in all children at some time but when it becomes 24/7 it is exhausting, especially with another baby (girl) who to our disbelief was also Lactose Intolerant although we identified this within 10 days of her birth and luckily her bowels were not as damaged. Below are some of the behavioural traits we experienced with H.

Unable to sit still/concentrate at all.

Jekyll & Hyde personality - aggressive/arsey/ argumentative yet also very affectionate.

Unable to process thoughts - excellent verbal skills but unable to speak in coherent sentences, often forgot what he was trying to say and got frustrated.

Very demanding, needing constant attention/interaction.

Unable to play on his own - would rather lie down, sleep or watch TV.

No imagination or concentration.

Lack of judgement - would run off regardless of safety issues -seemed "brave" but no self restraint - required constant supervision.

Would interrupt constantly - wanting instant response / attention.

Lack of appropriate social skills - very disruptive, unable to read "social clues"

Very emotional - up and down.

Refused to pick up a pencil or paints to draw (and hated trying to write/draw) having loved it at 12 mths old.

Very sensitive to noise/lights/stimulation - sensory over load distress.

Waking in night, very restless tossing & turning & teeth grinding or woke very early (5:00am) in an aggressive and grumpy mood.

Unable to listen or follow instructions even when making eye contact and repeating -as if it just didn't go in.

Would scare other children own age -preferred to play with older children.

Wanted to be in charge - as if he thought he was in control.

Manic activity/wired eg; shouting or singing very loudly.

After eating a small amount of a pink sugar mouse one Christmas sat rocking backwards and forwards in a world of his own for an hour like an autistic child. (Contained artificial colour sunset yellow).

Physical Symptoms

There were many physical symptoms, not that we realised at the time that these were nutritionally related, but the eczema and verrucas disappeared within one month of removing artificals, the others as we progressed through bio-medical interventions. This is a brief list;

Eczema on limbs - small white blisters - often raw and bleeding "chicken skin" - scaley, rough goose bumpy skin, black circle's under eyes, verrucas before the age of three, underweight for build - slow growth, cold sweats at night, distended stomach - full of Gas Unable to run without acid reflux/regurgitation "Withdrawal symptoms" after artificial colourants. Got very tired, cold and shivery even on a baking hot summer day.

The Path to Recovery

In May 04 with H aged 3 years 11 months we finally started to seriously link food to behaviour when H became intolerable after some organic orange juice and strawberries. I couldn't understand how such healthy foods could cause such aggressive behaviour. A friend mentioned that she knew other children for whom orange juice seemed to be a problem so I turned once again to the WWW and luckily found the HACSG. After spending over an hour on the phone with Sally and researching Feingold we eliminated all artificial colours and preservatives and within a few weeks the eczema and verrucas had cleared. We were on the right track at last.

We started keeping a VERY detailed food/behaviour diary and started trying positive parenting and other similar strategies for dealing with ADHD children. We then started an information and data gathering process that took us down many different paths, some of which were more use than others, most with a common central theme, but gave us different bits of information that enabled us to eventually determine our own path forward. This included "Allergy Induced Autism" (AIA) who explained about Autism Spectrum Disorders and digestive problems, Gluten and Caesin peptides, Dga (unlabelled MSG) and phenolsulfurtransferase issues. They suggested we did a Sunderland Urine test. AIA advocate a GF/CF diet but in our opinion this treats the symptoms but doesn't solve root cause. We had a consultation with Dr Natasha Campbell McBride who advised very strict Specific Carbohydrate

Diet, juicing (for natural enzymes) and digestive supplements such as probiotics, fish oils and vitamins/minerals. We did try Eye Q liquid but at this time H could not tolerate the natural lemon (citrus) flavour. Everything that Natasha Campbell McBride advocates is based on sound knowledge and research but we felt that removing all starches from a 4 yr old seemed a little extreme, and there had to be another way.

For completeness we decided we needed a conventional medical opinion and were referred to a Paedriatic Gastroenterologist at Gt Ormond Street who did traditional allergy tests (negative) but could offer no further help other than diet trials to see what foods he reacted to - but we knew that already! It seems they felt he wasn't physically ill enough to do anything else.

We were still bothered by WFIY highly Phenolic foods seemed to cause H such problems and whilst researching "Phenols" on the internet stumbled across something called "No-Phenol" a digestive enzyme for those who react to Phenols and decided it was worth a try. The product is made by a company in the USA specialising in digestive enzymes as an alternative to GF/CF for ASD children. So after further research/investigation we started using the No-Phenol Enzyme powder and saw an immediate improvement including the documented "Happy Child Effect". We were amazed that H was now able to eat highly Phenolic foods again with no reaction. At the same time we received the urine test results from Sunderland ARU that suggested a leaky gut, confirmation of what we had suspected all along. They suggested H go GF/CF and see an Autism specialist for a formal diagnosis.

After reading an excellent book by Karen DeFelice we decided that we would try the digestive enzyme path rather than GF/CF and after seeing with our own eyes the success of the No-Fenol enzyme it was worth exploring and if it failed we could always try GF/CF or the SCD. We introduced the two further Houston digestive enzymes (AFP and Zyme Prime) just before Christmas 04 and saw an immediate lifting of the "fog" in H's brain. A few weeks later we started adding Epsom Salts to the daily bath to help with phenolsulfurtransferase and these had a very calming effect.

In March we started high strength specialist probiotics as recommended by Natasha Campbell McBride and within one week H. was dry at night for the first time ever. Coincidence? We doubt it.

In May we tried Eye Q omega oils again - and three months on we have seen significant improvement in attention and concentration.

Where are we today?

All we can say is that H is now a TOTALLY different child, and this isn't just our opinion. Most of those who know H acknowledge that he is totally different, even those who initially thought he was just a lively intelligent boy can see the difference (and they didn't live with him!). His school have also noticed big improvements since he started in January 05. H was assessed by an Autism Spectrum Specialist Psychologist as showing ADHD traits but no longer presents these traits unless he has artificial colours/preservatives or MSG/Dga. (watch out for Marmite!) He is starting to catch up at school academically although we still suspect he is possibly dyslexic (inherited from father) and we are seeing him progress through many of the normal development stages that he seemed to have missed whilst his brain was not functioning properly. H is now able to eat virtually all foods with enzymes (including most dairy) but we avoid ALL artificials, hidden Free Glutumate (Dga) and hydrogenated fats. I won't pretend that it is easy, we still do a lot of home cooking, and can't just go on holiday or eat out without a lot of planning, but consider it well worth the sacrifice and effort. Physically H has grown at such a rate since we started enzymes and looks much healthier, no black circles, no bumpy skin, just rosy cheeks and a healthy glow.

H can still be challenging at times, but probably no more than a normal boy. The joy of having a calm affectionate child and being able to do normal family things is priceless, as is the mental state of two parents who were both on the verge of serious depression last year. To top it all, last week H was elected by his classmates to be their year representative as a school councellor - how especially proud we are of his achievement, something we could never have imagined a year ago.

Our hopes for the future?

Our ultimate aim is for a healed gut and a child able to eat normal healthy food, although I believe we will always avoid artificials and processed foods, but that can't be such a bad thing!

We are now confident that H is a healthy child who will be able to fulfil his potential and not end up as a tearaway teenager in trouble all the time.

We have found a path that helped our son and I would like to hope that this may be an option for other children with similar problems. Only by sharing our knowledge will we be able to see if our belief in healing the gut/brain link can provide a cure for others with behavioural difficulties. There are already many parents of ASD children using Bio-medical interventions with great success, and I would love to see a formal study into this with ADHD children.

Claire & Mark
30 September 2005

Brandy butter

I owe a great deal to the Hyperactive Children's Support Group (HACSG) although to date I have never met them, read any of their literature or been personally involved with them.

So how can it be that they have helped me and what have they done? Well I have to stretch my mind back to 1981, my fourteenth year and look at the very different picture my life and health was back then. I was very small for my age and not a particularly healthy example of a teenager despite my enthusiasm for sport.

I regularly had asthmatic fits and had to take my inhaler everywhere with me. On top of this I had very bad mouth ulcers, cold sores, was skinny as a rake and spent far too much time at the doctors being prodded, poked and peered at by a doctor with little idea of what was causing all this and probably hoped I would go away, grow up and stop bothering him. Repeat prescriptions came and went until finally the doctor announced to my mother (Ann) that he now had only one option...... ..STEROIDS.

Now looking back at this as a slightly wiser adult I see very much this path being prescribed week in week out for the new medication generation of attention deficit children. Doctors have a diagnosis, parents have a label and the medical profession can prescribe a container, bingo everyone's happy. However, many of them could be happier, I will explain! After the fateful diagnosis my mother's reaction to a startled doctor was 'not on my life will any child of mine go on steroids'. To say I am thankful for this reaction is an understatement

She had recently been reading a book called Chemical Victims by Richard Mackarness, which highlighted the problems in our food and farming with extensive use of chemicals and the effect this was having on our health. Then she saw a small flyer in a shop window for the HACSG in what must have been a serendipitous moment, or perhaps inevitable, knowing my mothers passion for shopping!

This was the turning point for a long suffering mother as suddenly she realised that she was not alone in this world and help was at hand.

After contacting the group and becoming friends with Val Kearney, a plan was hatched and the appropriate time to spring my surprise had to be decided. It happened one lunchtime when after a simple meal of eggs on toast my asthma fired up like an old church organ and I could barely speak through gasping breaths, something my wife would today like to replicate no doubt.

I had 5 full days of only mineral water and the most dreadful withdrawal symptoms, which shows that I had an excessive amount of chemicals in my body as I was racked with pain and had hallucinations despite never taking any illegal drugs (honestly). After this I was slowly reintroduced one foodstuff at a time and my reaction was measured through my pulse, pupils and general manner as any signs of extreme restfulness or fidgeting was a good pointer to an allergic reaction.

Well slowly but surely I developed a diet I could have, no cows milk, orange juice, wheat or nasty chemicals, my favourite things all gone, why could I not have been allergic to broad beans or belly pork life would have been so much simpler. My mother found organic butchers and goats milk which was no mean feat 25 years ago and set about making me simple wholesome food.

When I started my diet I was about 5 foot tall, skinny with blonde hair and a bad attitude. In just over a year I grew 10 inches my hair went dark brown and I filled out considerably, people who had not seen me for a while did not recognise me. However the real bonus was my health turned around almost immediately, I lost the asthma, which the doctors could not cure, and I no longer got mouth ulcers or cold sores. People say the bad attitude is definitely incurable though!

My mother was certainly happy with the transformation and a complete believer in the system of food elimination and following a right diet without unnecessary chemicals or irritants. She continued for many years to dispense advice to the willing, and sometimes the unwilling who would have preferred a pill to solve their problems, and today is an industrious 70 year old who gardens, cooks, quilts and still spends too much time staring in shop windows, but I can't complain.

To date I still follow my diet and have been able to reintroduce certain foodstuffs as my immune system has become stronger, I stand 6 foot 2 tall and apart from a dodgy knee from football I would say I am in excellent health. It is very much a way of life for me to eat well and on the occasions I do have something with a hidden nasty in it, I can still feel the effects of an allergic reaction.

Why the title Brandy Butter? Well the last Christmas before I started my diet I indulged in this delicacy and spoilt everyone's day by having a screaming fit and jumping up and down on the bathroom floor so much the chandeliers shook. Eventually I was pulled back through the window I was trying to climb out and had to be sat on to calm down. Thank the lord for Soya or I would have ruined so many more Christmases.

There must be thousands of people who have benefited from the time, advice and help that the wonderful volunteers from the HAGSG dispense so willingly, they were there in mine and my mother's time of need and without them my life may have been a much less happy story. It seems that the world

has changed a lot in 25 years and good food is definitely moving up the agenda both socially and politically, but much more remains to be done. For me though I am a firm believer and proof that you are what you eat.
Andrew Haley

Michael

We had a beautiful baby boy and such a blissfully peaceful first week. He was very hungry, feeding every couple of hours, but seemed to be a content, placid baby. This was in stark contrast to my daughter's first week of life - her crying from day one and terrible "colic", we later found out was due to cow's milk allergy and egg allergy. Now that she is 3½ she has an Epi-pen and remains on a cow's milk, dairy free, egg free and gluten free diet.

Unfortunately, the peace was shattered. At 2 weeks old, coinciding with my wound infection, M would cry inconsolably and solidly for 11 and sometimes up to 16 hours on a daily basis. He had become an insomniac and even if he managed to sleep from exhaustion, he would wake up after half an hour screaming as if someone had stuck a pin in him. The antibiotics I was given for my wound infection were blamed for his diarrhoea and projectile vomiting. Once they were out of his system, his projectile vomiting stopped but M was still suffering from diarrhoea, daily vomiting and inconsolable crying. He also had an umbilical hernia and hydrocele.

I continued breast feeding but cut out milk and dairy products in my diet. M was diagnosed with severe colic and reflux and we were given medicines to help with this. Unfortunately, M did not seem to be able to tolerate the medicines for his reflux. We started counting the days until he would be 4 months old as traditionally this is when colic is supposed to subside. I tried Nutramigen and Neocate milks both of which gave him puffy eyes and rashes and seemed to make him more "windy" and irritable. We also had great difficulty trying to bottle feed him as he was sick after feeds and often refused them.

I was told that "he couldn't possibly be allergic to these hypoallergenic milks". However, after a hospital stay at 10 weeks old, we moved onto Modular Neocate (Neocate milk without soy bean oil) and after 2 weeks he gradually became a little more settled. I stopped breast feeding and we were hopeful that things would be better in the New Year. M had already endured so many things as a young baby:- severe colic, reflux, constant vomiting, hernia, hydrocele, bouts of diarrhoea, bronchiolitis and milk and medicine intolerances.

The New Year brought more angst. M suffered gastroenteritis. He lost a lot of weight and was diagnosed with "acute or chronic hypokalaemia" as his Potassium levels were so low. M was given Potassium and Sodium supplements but over time these made his excema, especially that on his face, flare up and his colic worse. Our chemist suggested that M was probably sensitive to the hydroxybenzoates in the supplements.

By the age of 6 months M had been hospitalised three times and we were now reluctantly back on Nutramigen milk. It felt as if no-one knew how to help him and we felt particularly isolated waiting for "time" to help him. In spite of everything, M still looked "well covered" and "healthy" managing to smile at doctors and nurses. However, his inconsolable crying and insomnia continued and he started head-banging.

When he was 6 months old we started to wean him on a milk, egg, soya and gluten-free diet. I thought this would be easy as we had already done the same for my daughter. M seemed to be sensitive to different fruit and vegetables, with rashes appearing and disappearing, he would sometimes sweat profusely and was still very unsettled. His diarrhoea got worse again. He would have good days and bad days. Sometimes he would do such huge vomits you would never have thought possible from a baby. Night time was worse than ever - despite a good bed time routine and M falling asleep on his own, after half an hour he would sit bolt-upright with his eyes shut, screaming - this would happen sometimes up to 20 times throughout the night. Sleep deprivation was affecting us all and M's head banging got so bad that we moved him into a travel cot as it had soft sides. To add to his problems, M now had excema all over his body, chicken-pox, a perforated ear drum, 3 ear infections in 4 months and virus after virus as he continually had symptoms of a runny nose, rattly chest and loose stools.

Just as we looked to alternative methods to help our daughter, we took M to the same cranial osteopath. He has been particularly helpful and supportive and we firmly believe that he has helped with M's bronchiolitis, reflux and ear infections. It is so good to see someone who is supportive, objective and most importantly, takes a holistic approach. He told us that he believed that M was physically so much stronger now and his reflux was getting better all the time and we joked that I must follow my "gut feeling" about M's diet. He thought that there was something chemically, not physically wrong with M.

At 14 months old M had endured so much and had only had 3 nights' sleep (2 from exhaustion and one from being given a mild sedative when he was utterly miserable). I became desperate, not knowing whom to turn to, his behaviour was distressing to see, one minute he would be playing quite happily with his toys, the next minute, his face would flush and he would cry inconsolably, banging his head on the floor or cupboard door - anything. These tantrums were horrific and inexplicable.

As M had by now regained his weight and was looking "well", we were told that there would be no more investigations until he was 18 months old. With M screaming in the background I called the HACSG because I thought they might be able to help us with M and his food intolerances. I was given so much support, help and advice. M had remained on his milk, egg, soya and gluten free diet but we were giving him raisins and apple puree on a daily basis. M is still on his milk, egg, soya and gluten free diet but in addition we have cut out salicylates (aspirin found naturally in some fruit and vegetables) and we are following the Ben Feingold diet plan. A hair analysis showed that M was very low in Zinc and Magnesium. He has been diagnosed with a leaky gut/malabsorption problem, so we are giving him pure Zinc and Magnesium supplements.

It is so much more than a coincidence that after one week, M slept through the night for the first time (and has continued sleeping through the night since then). His day-time irritability/tantrums and head banging have stopped and friends and family describe him as a "different little boy". He can now concentrate on playing and is so much more settled and content. We cannot thank Sally Bunday enough for the best Christmas present ever!

My advice to other parents would be to follow your gut feeling and not give up on finding help for your child if they are inwardly suffering despite "looking well"!

On being a parent of a ADHD child...

Having survived until my son has reached the age of 19, I can now look back and wonder where I got the strength and will power to carry on but also to be proud of the son that I have.

The problems started when my son started to walk. He had always been an inquisitive and knowing child. Having started to talk at 5 months with the word 'flower', from then on things were never quiet. But I can say that we never had a problem with his sleeping. He would not go to sleep until about 10.00 pm but would sleep through until 8.00 am most days. But at 14 months I found I had a child that acted like a wind up toy, the moment his feet hit the floor he was off. I sought medical advice only to be told that I had a highly intelligent over active child and I should be grateful. I put up with this until he was three and asked for a referral to a specialist. I was referred to a child psychologist who diagnosed hyperkinises. We had noticed that certain foods made him worse so we tried to avoid orange, chocolate and fizzy drinks. We were then referred to Great Ormond Street Hospital and after several visits over the next two years it was recommended that my son take Ritalin. I was not happy with this. I became aware of HACSG and the Feingold diet.

I started to try this diet and things became better. I mentioned this on our next visit to the hospital and the professor took a dim view of dietary approach and suggested that we no longer needed to attend the hospital. My son continued to take Ritalin for about 6 months then all of a sudden he said 'I don't want to take those pills any more. It makes me feel like my arms, legs aren't attached to my body and I don't behave any better do I?' I had to agree and decided to go the diet route. It was not easy trying additional therapy along the way. This included stroking with brushes and the more successful cranial osteopathy.

But the biggest break through came when my son met Vicky Colquhoun for the first time. She could not believe how 'hyper' he was or how I managed to cope. She suggested a visit to Bio-Labs for tests. This my son really enjoyed as he could see the isotope travelling through his stomach on the computer screen. We were to learn that his stomach did not produce the correct amount of hydrochlauric acid therefore the required nutrients were not being extracted from his food. This was a breakthrough. Although getting him to take a hydrochloric acid tablet was difficult. We had already learnt of the effect of sugar, monosodium glutamate, additives and preservatives and exhaust emissions. To be honest at one stage I felt like giving up.

All this time I readily admitted that my son was a problem and to his detriment I took the side of his educators. His classmates soon learnt that it was easy to wind him up and he would be blamed not them. I would try to warn people of the effect if they allowed him things that would set him off. But alas there are far too many people who think it is cruel to stop children from having things they perceive children like. I was accused of bad parenting. I tried to encourage his creative side and steered clear of organised things like cubs and scouts, although he did enjoy fencing. All the time I tried to keep to the Feingold diet.

When he was old enough, with the encouragement of his maths teacher, he started on the Duke of Edinburgh Award Scheme. I cannot say it was an easy journey but it was most enjoyable and at the age of 17 he achieved the D of E Gold. He has gone on to be involved locally with the Scouts, pay back for his community service on the Bronze DofE Award, and is about to become assistant leader for the local troop. He is at college working on a HMD course in Computing for Practitioners hoping eventually to obtain a degree.

My sanity has been saved over the years by knowing that HACSG were at the end of the telephone, giving me support and advice. I am eternally grateful to them. I am also grateful that I was able to see and accept my son's problems and try to deal with them. Parents who are unable to see that their children are behaving in a socially unacceptable way do no favours to

are behaving in a socially unacceptable way do no favours to themselves or their children. Quite often it takes just simple steps to rectify. I was unfortunate that my son had such a high degree of sensitivity. It is not looking for problems when you just think about how they behave after a bar of chocolate or a fizzy drink you can be saving them from themselves.

For 30 years the Hyperactive Children's Support Group has worked tirelessly to bring to the attention of successive Governments and the medical profession the effect that the excessive amount of additives and preservatives in food is having our children's well being and they have only just managed to scratch the surface. Unfortunately the medical profession still offer a medical cosh more readily than a look at diet and nutrition.

In conclusion I would say that the effects of ADHD any many fold and each child's reaction is different. There are many examples in life where people have managed to cope with the effects. But ADHD does not go away in adult life; one just learns to cope with it. My son can now predict his behaviour when he has eaten or smelt certain things. But even he is caught out occasionally. Aerosol deodorants are one of the worst!

Nicholas

Very soon after our first son, Nicholas, was born on the 29th June 1976, we knew we were going to have a difficult time but just how difficult and traumatic we just could not have imagined at that time.

The "professionals" then had probably not accepted that outside influences could have such a devastating effect on a baby and that it must be down to the strictness of the parents to educate, train and control their offspring, firmly placing the onus on us.

After many years of non-stop screaming, behavioural problems and on our part, total exhaustion, we tried enlisting the help of our then GP and the paediatric Consultant at Colchester General Hospital. Our second son, Simon born 29 September 1977, fortunately did not have the same problems but because Nick required 24-hour care Simon tended to get, and feel, neglected no matter how much we tried to avoid this.

We knew there was more to Nick's problem than us being bad parents and felt that pouring Calpol into him and giving him a good smacking, as advised by our GP, or being prescribed medicine by the Consultant that contained colourings that made him even worse, yes worse, was just not on. We changed our GP and left the Consultant to it.

By a stroke of good fortune we saw a Panorama programme on TV with Dr H. Jolly showing behavioural problems of children and connecting them to their diet. A few days later an article in the local newspaper on 6th January 1986, followed by another one on the 24th (we still have copies), allowed us to trace the HACSG from this and we joined the local group. It was fantastic to find we were not alone, in fact far from it, but it changed our lives and made us feel human beings again after 9 years and some frightening uncontrolled near misses that could have ended Nick's life.

Once we had religiously undertaken the Feingold diet, in which we all took part so as not to make Nick feel different, the change once we had found the triggers was dramatic to say the least. Not just for Nick but for his Dad who unbeknown had milk intolerance as well and within three days of giving up the favourite pint of milk a day found that it was no longer normal to have blinding migraines or spend considerable time recovering in the toilet. What a bonus!

The experience that Nick had at school could not be switched off over night and because the teachers could not get to grips with this rapidly changing child, they had written him off to the special needs class. His mother decided to take a child psychology course and also a course run locally with the education department on how to teach 7-11 year olds, specifically to help Nick understand his lessons. It was at this stage that we also found out that he had hearing dyslexia from the ENT Specialist, which meant he could not hear the pronunciation of words causing further difficulties for him. Mum then spent every evening with Nick helping him to read and "hear" his words. She also found the system worked with our youngest son, who was also now showing signs of disruptive behaviour and lack of concentration.

As the schools did not appear to be interested in resolving problems for children like Nick, it became evident that someone had to be on the inside not only to watch over him but to help all the other students that we had since identified as having a problem. Dad became a School Governor and gradually educated as many others who would take time to listen and through this enlisted the assistance of our future MP for Colchester, Bob Russell, who helped protect me from some more powerful non-believers in the Education Department. We did have some success in preventing unnecessary exclusions from School but did see some of the children identified as allergic fall by the wayside and end up in prison because the parents weren't committed to the cause to help them.

We even infiltrated the catering department for a time getting a more friendly diet introduced into Schools, but unfortunately not for long enough and Jamie Oliver was then probably still at school himself. Nick proved his tutors very wrong when he not only came top in several subjects at exam time but also won one of only four engineering apprenticeships out of 800 applicants at a very big engineering company.

Once qualified, he went on to develop many of the car diesel engines for the big car manufacturers whilst working for Lotus Engineering.

Nick is now a family man and runs his own successful heating and plumbing business in Norfolk. He is also halfway through his plans to set up equestrian training stables, which will be operated by his wife.

Thank God we ignored the education and medical experts!! You may also be interested in the fact that we found the regime also helped some people we came into contact with by improving hearing dyslexia.

We are so proud of what has been achieved with the help of the HACSG, although we must reiterate that it can only work with commitment from all parties over as long as it takes, and that you should go by your gut instincts, not taking "no" as an answer.

Yours sincerely,

John & Pat Budd

Spencer

Spencer was born on 22nd June 1991. From five days old he was a very miserable baby. He cried continually, did not sleep well and was prone to projectile vomiting. He was breast-fed until the age of four months.

His mother sought advice from her doctor, the clinic, the health visitor, etc., but apart from reassuring her that there was nothing major wrong with him, none of the advice made Spencer any easier to handle.

As he grew older his behaviour became even more difficult to tolerate. He seemed to cry all the time, was permanently thirsty, had violent tantrums, was destructive, restless, unable to concentrate for more than a few seconds on anything, and was very aggressive. His small sister was covered in bruises from his punches and he would lash out at anybody or anything, including the dog, that got in his way. He would not make eye contact, often did not appear to hear when spoken to and his behaviour was so anti-social and uncontrollable that his mother's friends asked her not to bring him to visit.

His mother was in despair. She took him to see a child psychologist and tried out the advice given - all to no avail! Spencer's behaviour was destroying the family and as you looked into that sullen little face, filled with anger and misery, the future looked very bleak indeed.

In 1994 Paula mentioned the problem to an osteopath she was attending and he recommended that she take Spencer to a Children's Osteopathic Centre in London, where they specialised in helping children with behavioural problems. Paula took Spencer for several treatments and he was a very difficult patient to treat! He refused to lie on the table or to keep still in fact, finding humour in a very difficult situation, his treatments used to remind me, (his grandmother,) of the end sequence of a Benny Hill show, with about six of us chasing him between all the other treatment couches.

However, with patience, the osteopaths were able to work on him briefly each session. There was some improvement in his behaviour but clearly this was not the whole answer. It was during one of the later treatments that the osteopaths decided to test Spencer for sensitivity to dairy produce and to sugar. They found a marked intolerance to sugar and suggested that he might also be reacting to the chemical additives found in many foodstuffs of the day.

This was the turning point! Much research followed, culminating in the discovery of the Hyperactive Children's Support Group. The advice we received was invaluable.

As our understanding of the effects of sugar, additives and salicylates grew, it was rather mortifying to realise that much of the suffering endured in the first four years of Spencer's life -mostly, of course, by Spencer in the discomfort, misery and punishment received for acts he couldn't control, was actually caused by the 'poison' (for Spencer) being fed to him unwittingly by those who loved him most.

A list of 'safe' foods was drawn up and Spencer's diet was modified. The result was astounding! Within four days of withdrawing all sugar, additives and some juices from Spencer's diet there was a mini-miracle! From the miserable, aggressive, destructive child that he used to be, emerged a delightful, affectionate little boy with a wonderful smile. He was loving, happy (most of the time!) - could now sit still and listen to stories, or play games, or watch television. Most of the aggression disappeared. The amazing thing was how he accepted totally the changes in his diet. He never resented the fact that his sister could have sweets and he couldn't, and in fact, he used to check with adults as to whether they were giving him something that contained sugar! It appeared that he appreciated how much better he felt when not eating the wrong things. One mouthful was enough to trigger a hyperactive reaction. Within twenty minutes the old symptoms would reappear and could last for up to a week!

On the advice of HACSG, Spencer's diet was supplemented with the addition of Essential Fatty Acids, initially in the form of Evening Primrose Oil, and then, when the product came on the market, with Eye Q, which combines fish oils and Evening Primrose Oil. There is no doubt that these oils benefit the consumer enormously, aiding concentration, learning, memory and mood.

At the time of writing this story, Spencer is now coming up to sixteen. His sensitivity to some foodstuffs is still apparent. He is aware that chocolate and an overdose of sugar, monosodium glutamate and fizzy drinks can give him migraine headaches and make him moody and emotional. On the whole he avoids them. As a small child his fine motor skills were affected and he still has almost illegible handwriting. However, he has grown into a delightful young man (proud grandmother speaking), is currently taking his GCSEs, and has a college course and future career mapped out. How different it might have been!!

Spencer has generously allowed his story to be an illustration in HACSG workshops, the subject of a radio programme, a television interview, several magazine articles, a fun CD and a cartoon to help little children understand why their diet is being altered. As he enters adulthood this is probably the last time his story will be told. However, he goes forward armed with all the knowledge he needs to cope easily with his food intolerance problems. He is one of the lucky ones!

Monty

M was not a particularly unsettled baby and was generally quite well but as he became a toddler he was always "on the go" flitting from one activity to another, needing a lot of one to one attention from his mum to keep him happy. She said it wasn't a problem to her, that was just the way he was. He slept very little and mum mould often be up with him in the middle of the night. During my routine health visiting contacts I discussed this with her on several occasions but she didn't consider it a problem.

When M was two and a half years old his baby brother was born and since mum was awake in the night to feed the baby she didn't consider that M being up as well was anything to worry about and carried on as usual. I don't know how she managed with so little sleep but with hindsight I think she was probably a little hyperactive herself.

The change came when baby brother at the age of ten months developed quite severe eczema and asthma. The hospital dietitian suggested to mum that it would be a good idea to remove all food additives from his diet, particularly colourings and preservatives. Since mum did not want to be cooking different meals for him from the rest of the family they all went on the same diet.

Mum came to see me in clinic and told me what had happened. The babys condition had improved dramatically which pleased her immensely but she wanted to tell me about M. He was much calmer generally, had a greatly increased attention span and was actually sleeping 11 hours at night. "I never really understood why you were worried about him until now" she said, "I never realised how bad he was until he stopped being".

There was an amusing incident following this. M, during his hyperactive period, had been in the habit when coming to the GP surgery of shunting the rows of stacking chairs with a distinctive noise of banging and scraping which could be heard from our office in the back of the building so we always knew when he was in. This stopped when he went on the diet but one day when he was four years old we heard it again and went out to investigate. Sure enough it was M. "What happened?", I asked his mother.

She laughed and said that she had got so used to his diet that she had forgotten to tell anyone when he started having school dinners and needed a note from the doctor to keep him off the additives. It wasn't too difficult for them, they just had to stop the gravy and the pink custard, everything else was cooked from fresh ingredients.

From a HACSG professional member

During a visit to a new baby the mother mentioned to me that her older child, who was three and a half years old, was prone to outbursts of impulsive and sometimes aggressive behaviour for no apparent reason and at random times. During the ensuing discussion she supplied her own answer to the problem when she said "Take the other day for instance, he had been so good and quiet all morning that when we went out to the park I bought him some Smarties as a reward but then soon afterwards he became totally unmanageable".

I asked how often he had sweets and it appeared it was very rarely so that didn't account for the entire problem so we discussed his usual eating pattern. The foods that she told me he ate regularly were actually very sound nutritious meals and I thought perhaps I was barking up the wrong tree until I asked about between meal snacks. "Oh yes", she said "he does have fizzy drinks and loves savoury snacks like Quavers and Monster Munch". I suggested that she stick to giving him plain crisps and if she had to give him fizzy drinks to stick to an occasional 7up.

When I saw her again two weeks later she said that she couldn't believe the difference changing just those two food items had made and she was now persuading all friends and relatives not to give him "junk" without checking with her first.

I had been asked by a colleague to see a mum with a three year old child who she suspected had ADHD but had an unsympathetic GP who didn't want to know. I did a home visit and spent about an hour and a half discussing the situation and explaining the Feingold Diet. She agreed to try it and rang me a month later to express her gratitude and say that the situation was now under control. I heard from her again when the child began attending the local school nursery class in the mornings and although he was still following his diet he had started "kicking off " in school. The nursery teacher thought it was a behaviour problem but mum felt there was more to it than that and asked if I could go and talk to the school.

I met with the teacher and the nursery nurse on a Monday morning, before the children arrived, to discuss the problems. They understood about the additive free diet although they seemed a little sceptical, but as he did not eat during school time didn't think that it was relevant. I tried to explain to them that children who have ADHD may also react to other environmental factors and the sort of things that could cause a reaction and could tell from their response that they were now beginning to consider me as some sort of crank. They could not, they said, do anything to control the environment. The furniture, fabrics and cleaning materials used in the building were all outside their control and they were not going to disrupt their routines by allowing him a little time in the fresh air when he was getting "wound up"as this would be seen by the other children as a reward. There was in fact a very noticeable, although not unpleasant, smell to the building.

Just as I felt I was fighting a losing battle two other members of staff arrived and one of them went into the kitchen to put the kettle on. She started to sneeze and said "Oh, here we go again". I asked her to explain the remark and she said that within a short time of arriving at work on a Monday she would start sneezing and that by the end of the week she would have a mild sore throat and be quite sinusy. The problem went away on a weekend and had started at the beginning of term. I asked if anyone else had similar problems and it seemed that several of them had similar, although less severe symptoms.

I now suggested to them that they might have "Sick building syndrome" and that as this was their reaction to their environment, the childs reaction was a return of his hyperactivity. The penny suddenly seemed to drop and they asked what they could to about it. Having previously attended a seminar on the subject, I suggested that new furniture and a new carpet recently installed might be the cause of the problem as they gave off fumes and that good ventilation and a few broadleaved plants such as cheese plants would help to clear the atmosphere.

Mum rang me about three weeks later and said that my suggestion had been taken up, half a dozen large green plants had appeared in the classroom, and as the smell was gradually lessening so were her child's outbursts.

Rachel & Holly

I would like to thank you for all the support and help for myself and my daughter Holly, who is now nine.

I was a poorly child and cut out certain foods such as E102, Quinoline yellow, chocolate, white bread, Frosties, sugar puffs and cow's milk. Back then in the seventies people and doctors thought it was mad to cut out such things and it had no connection with food whatsoever.

I remember the days whilst ill off school drinking Lucozade and my head spinning, body twitching and not being able to keep still. I was happy but frustrated. I loved art but could only scribble because my head was so busy. I couldn't switch off or sleep, I was exhausted. One day whilst off school ill me and my mother watched a program presented by Ester Ranson who tackled the subject on certain food colourings being able to make certain people ill i.e. food intolerances. This is the point when my foods got restricted and I started to improve.

When I was 29 I had Holly. At the time I was suffering from ME Asthma and Eczema, Holly was breast feed for 10 months after that she had a Soya formula then goats milk. She was always irritable and hard to settle down with Eczema flare ups. Apart from ointments we had no support or direction forward. Just before Holly's birthday she had her first fit. She stopped breathing and had CPR, then was hospitalised, no cause was found.

From then onwards she would fit regularly every six weeks her temperature would go up, her ears and head would ache, she was always sensitive to noise and light. After she fitted she wouldn't be able to walk or talk properly for up to two weeks. In 2000 she had Pnuemoccoical Septicaemia and fitted for 72 minutes. She didn't wake up for nine hours.

In between fits Holly was extremely hyperactive and had certain rituals to perform before venturing out. She always had a certain small charm she had to have on her at all times. She would stand at the top of the stairs screaming holding her head but wouldn't let you near her; she would run off the landing as if there were no steps, bump into doors. Whilst shopping I held on to her at all times because she would wander off in a dolly day dream. She would crave certain foods and wouldn't be able to stop eating them. And not be able to understand a simple instruction. It was totally exhausting day & night, I was a single parent when Holly was 18 months old, with ME, but had a very supportive mother . We had to help Holly somehow.

One day I discovered HACSG. I desperately phoned Sally who understood Holly's problems! I sat and cried. Sally posted bundles of information and an appointment to the HACSG where we saw Dr. Clive Jones. Holly was taken off all dairy, wheat, food colourings and preservatives and sodium benzoates. From there we saw Dr. Tettenborn who diagnosed Holly with autistic induced food intolerances. She was put on a Sugar & Yeast free diet along with the other foods plus supplements of zinc, magnesium and calcium along with EFA's and probiotics which we had made up privately, because the NHS probiotic contained colourings and preservatives. After a while Holly improved immensely. She was calm, happy, would laugh and sing, forgot her rituals, she could run and look people in the eyes and her sensitivities to noise and light reduced and she had a nights sleep. Her eyes didn't have dark circles underneath and she looked healthy and her fits stopped. They were caused by a toxic overload from the foods. Holly is now nine and a picture of health and very happy in a main stream school. She recognizes what foods to avoid and avoids them where possible.

Unfortunately some medical professionals still don't want to believe the connection of foods and chemicals to a poorly child and all the problems it can cause. I have lost count the number of times doctors have tried prescribing medicines with colourings and preservatives in and saying it won't harm Holly. Also judges have the same view that unless medically proven through blood tests (which can only show positive to allergies) foods can't have such detrimental effects on a child, and the other parent has the right to feed the child anything they wish whilst in their care, resulting in a relapse and a poorly child when they come home a very frustrating and long battle to get them better again for the next visit. The problem that Holly and I still have. Without Sally and the HACSG, Holly could have suffered permanent irreversible damage and a life of misery and suffering. It may look daunting to the parents and children who look at changes in diet, etc. but you and your child's life will be much happier and more fulfilling if you persevere. Thank you Sally and HACSG for helping Holly and all the ongoing support in the black days and present, also my Mum who believed in us.

I wish you all the luck in the world with your book and the future for HASCG, please except my support and donation.

Yours truly,

Rachel Giles and Holly x x x x x

Jonathan

Jonathan was born by emergency caesarean a few weeks overdue and weighed 8lb 7ozs. He had quite bad colic as a baby but was healthy apart from that.

At two he developed eczema and no matter how much cream I used it did little to help him. The stronger creams would help and clear his skin but as soon as they were stopped, his eczema reappeared (these creams were only recommended to be used for short spells at a time).

I heard about the HACSG when he was three and got a lot of useful information. I decided to get a hair analysis done to see what foods could be causing sensitivities and also decided to see a homeopath. His skin improved gradually and his sleep also improved.

He has always been active, however I was concerned with his behaviour and when he was nearly five I tried to get some advice. I was unable to find the advice or information I needed so approached the HACSG to see if they had any answers. Again they provided me with research, information and ideas for me to consider. I decided to try the Feingold Diet and was amazed with the response. I still felt that he was sensitive to certain foods and arranged for Dr McDonough to do a food sensitivity test. This confirmed the foods that he was more sensitive to. Again the response was amazing. I decided to read up a little on nutrition and how the gut worked. I decided to also make adjustments to what foods were eaten together and when they were eaten. I feel this helps him and does not put a burden on his digestive system.

He also has Omega 3, Zinc and maybe a mineral supplement but does not have these all the time (usually in spells).

He is now seven and I thought I would get his spine checked by a chiropractor. He has actually got a slight curve in his spine causing one leg to be longer than the other (could have been since birth! and curve could be causing pressure on the nerves). After a bit of realignment his legs are now level and he seems very relaxed after each session.

I still see the Homeopath regularly but feel he has really benefited from the above approaches. He is not an easy child, always eager, full of energy, very bright, very caring and also very sensitive but these approaches have helped him over the years.

Because of his eagerness he can be quite disruptive at school and because we have to have quite strict rules at home I thought he would enjoy something where he could be himself. I found a good Drama school locally, with an amazing teacher who allowed the children to develop themselves whilst having very good control over them. It is only an after schools club but after the first few sessions he settled in to it very well and enjoys it immensely.

He has an amazing memory but lacks concentration and being focussed. I am going to follow up the article on Brain Gym activities in the recent HACSG journal.

Simon

In 1986 Simon was born and within 6 months was suffering from eczema. I had read somewhere that this can sometimes be caused by diary products so removed all such products from his diet with amazing results. Concerned that he may not be getting enough calcium, I contacted my health visitor who gave me a list of other calcium rich foods and suggested that I contact someone she knew who could, advise me further on food allergies. She wrote Val Kearney's number on the top of the list she handed me.

Because Simon's eczema disappeared at that time I did not contact Val and it wasn't until 5 years later that I came across her again. By this time I had Rebecca who I had kept away from diary products and she showed no signs of eczema. However, Simon was by now asthmatic and had eczema flare ups despite being off dairy products.

In 1991 I was branch chairman for the local NCT group and went along to the monthly talks to show support even if they were not relevant to me. On this particular occasion it was to hear Val Kearney speak about the local Hyperactive Children's Support Group. My children were the complete opposite of hyperactive - they whined constantly, were slow to talk, very shy and clingy. I sat and listened to Val speak about the symp-toms of food allergy and was only half listening to all the hyperactivity systems when she started to describe my own children's behaviour - whiney, clingy, shy, constant thirst, slow to talk. Suddenly I sat up and started taking notice. Val is a very compelling speaker and I totally believed every word she said. That night 1 went home and cleared the cupboards and fridge of all processed foods especially the orange squash that Rebecca was constantly drinking. Next day I was down at the health food shop re-stocking my cupboards with additive free food and the local green grocer finding all the green veg I could get.

Within a week both children had been allergy tested by Val, using Kinesiology. I then took it as a personal challenge to find alternatives to all the food the children were so used to - tomatoes, oranges, shop bread and biscuits/cakes etc. With the help of Val and other members of the HACSG group I soon put together a list of a variety of new meals to feed the family.

We even started making our own soda bread and normal bread. The first week of the new regime was hell! Rebecca had tantrums worse than before when she could not have orange squash and Simon cried and clung more than normal. But with support from Val and others at the support group meetings we got through it and within 2 weeks my children had become little angels. They were truly delightful to take out and no longer clung to me. 1 could actually leave a room without them following me. This meant I could at last go to the loo by myself and shut the door! In combination with the diet, we used homeopathy and aromatherapy to help Simon's asthma which meant we no longer had to rely on the sugar enhanced concoction from the doctor to stop his attacks. Simon's speech improved dramatically and finally Rebecca stopped her tantrums,

When Rebecca was about 8 years old her tantrums started again and the school contacted me about her behaviour in class. Up to then she had been a model pupil. But she suddenly started to play up and couldn't sit still or concentrate. I couldn't understand why this was happening as her diet was fine. Then one day I smelt strawberries on her breath and the story all came out. A new neighbour had a girl about Rebecca's age who was giving her sweets. I had a chat with her mum and explained why Rebecca could not have sweets. Once off the sweets, Rebecca's behaviour went back to normal and I think it made an impression on the teacher who gave up eating chocolate (which gave her migraines) in support of Rebecca.

Because I decided that I would also eat the same food as the children, and so would my husband John, there were other benefits with the new diet too. My PMT disappeared and both John and I felt so much better with more energy. Along with the children we rarely get colds and have never had a day off work through illness. I even gave up smoking, eventually!

Simon is now 20 years old and in his second year at University studying to be an IT System Manager. He tries to maintain a healthy diet (not easy with a house full of lads eating take aways) and knows how to cook 'proper' food. He has not had an asthma attack for about 10 years now and although he does get the occasional mild eczema flare up he knows it is down to him to look at his diet when this happens. He is confident, great at organising and is achieving excellent results.

Rebecca has grown into a beautiful woman, with a wonderful, outgoing personality of her own. She doesn't drink, smoke or do drugs because she is so aware of her own body and the effect that food and other substances can have on it. She is studying for her A levels at the moment and has been accepted by the leading university to become a Sports Therapist. Both children are happy and confident and without the HACSG they would be totally different and I am convinced they would not have achieved what they have without the help and support this wonderful group has given me over the years, 1 still spread the word to anyone I meet and hope that I may have helped others too through the example of my children.

Although I wish the HACSG the very best for the future I hope that one day it will no longer be needed because everyone is eating good, healthy food free from commercial junk.

Rosalind

Miles, age sixteen

Tony

Born in 1972 after a 43-week pregnancy and a quick and easy labour, Tony was one of only two boy babies in the maternity ward, and was by far the biggest and noisiest of all the babies there. We were proud, first-time parents. We brought him home after a week, and it was then that the real trouble started. We soon realised that he screamed at every sound, every movement, and every chink of light. He screamed when being bathed, when being changed, and when being wheeled along in his pram. He screamed at everybody and everything apart from me. I had to lay him in his cot on his tummy (as one was recommended to do in those days), before he could finally settle down and drift off to sleep. I also learned to change him in this position it kept him quieter.

He suffered terribly from colic, and would scream all and every evening, often bringing up his milk. I was feeding him myself, but couldn't conceive that my own milk didn't agree with him. I couldn't establish a regular feeding pattern for him he would refuse to feed when it was time for him to do so, and then he would wake up a few hours later, screaming his head off. I began to wonder why I had given up a good job in order to become a mother!

When Tony started teething, more trouble ensued. He would develop bronchitis with every second tooth, and pass it on to me, then on to his father. We were constantly at the doctor's surgery, rapidly swelling the profits of the pharmaceutical companies. Tony's father and I were getting to the end of our tether under the strain of it all. We took him along to as many professionals as we could find doctors, paediatricians, dietitians but all said that there was nothing wrong with him.

At eleven months of age, Tony began to reject all foods except for bread, dry biscuits, apples, bananas and fruit juices. Everything else he would chuck on to the floor in a rage. Eventually, he started eating a few more things, like chips, sausages and so on, but his behaviour was becoming very challenging. He would throw tantrums when he didn't get his own way (he had a will of iron) and began to upset our neighbours and alienate our friends by causing damage to their belongings and property. When he was just two, my mother died suddenly, plunging us all into utter despair. By now my father and parents-in-law were well into their seventies, and requiring more help from me than I could expect from them. I could barely cope.

Tony's physical development had been slow, and he had taken ages to sit up, crawl and walk. I was still desperately trying to potty-train him at three years of age when his sister Louise was born. He was sick all night, so that my husband was unable to stay with me to witness her birth, and indeed I only just reached the hospital in time after changing Tony's bedding yet again. He was insanely jealous of his baby sister (whom he called "YOUR baby") and she was lucky to survive some of the things he did to her. By contrast, she was a text-book baby. We knew only then that the problems were Tony's and not due to our incompetence!

When Tony reached four, he started at the little prep school up the road. They were pretty strict there, classes were small, and one of the teachers was a friend of mine. However, because his behaviour was still "at times unacceptable", we took Tony to our local child guidance centre. There we were told that he would be lucky to get one O-level, so poor was his concentration. However, we had always thought that underneath it all he had a good brain, waiting to be unlocked, and so we then took him to see an educational psychologist. He was immediately diagnosed as "hyperactive".

I decided to investigate this "hyperactivity", of which I hadn't heard before, and soon made contact with Sally Bunday, who had just set up a support group for parents in our situation. By this time Tony's teacher was recommending speech therapy for possible dyslexia. I immediately embarked on the transfer to the Feingold Diet which Sally was recommending, something which wasn't easy in those days and which took several months to achieve. However, I soon found that Tony was becoming much more manageable, and heard no more about dyslexia from the school. He finally became dry at night (he was now 5½), stopped biting his fingernails and toenails, and, if I did have to smack him, it would register, whereas previously he would just have sat and laughed at me. We were all on the Feingold Diet by now, and feeling much healthier, more energetic and more able to cope with things.

Every spring we would visit cousins in Worthing (some of the few people who would still put up with us) and I would go along and visit Sally. In February 1982, when Tony was 9, Sally gave me a free sample of Evening Primrose Oil, which she said was proving beneficial to hyperactive children in trials that were taking place. I had heard of this oil in Prevention Magazine (where I had also just read an article about the Feingold Diet) and I was keen to try it. The result was astonishing.

Tony looked bright-eyed, and developed colour in his cheeks and shine in his hair, and a clear complexion. His memory improved, and he became more organised. His handwriting, too, stopped being a scratchy scrawl and became fluent and rounded. His monthly assessments at school showed improvement in everything except Maths. I went up to see the Maths master, who told me that Tony had suddenly become so clever that he would finish his exercises in the first ten minutes and spend the rest of the lesson disrupting the other boys. He agreed to give Tony much harder exercises, and the problem was solved.

When Tony was 13, he gained a place in the upper ability band of one of the country's foremost public schools. He obtained such high marks in the entrance exam that we were told that he could have tried for a scholarship had the prep school known several years earlier that he would turn out to be so clever. He sailed through his teens without problems, made many friends at the school, gained 13 O-Levels and 3 A-Levels, all at top grades, and went on to university, where he graduated in Law with Italian, spending a whole year in Italy. He has had several interesting jobs since then, each one an improvement on the last in terms both of responsibility and of remuneration. He is tall and handsome, has a happy, sunny disposition, is hugely popular and is a loving, generous son and brother.

Tony is now a successful investment banker and has recently married. He and his wife are very good cooks and are very health-conscious, both religiously taking their Omega 3 and Omega 6 and various vitamin supplements. His sister, too, is equally successful and health-conscious, is also married, and, as I write, is expecting our first grandchild. And, not to be outdone, Tony and his wife have since announced that they are expecting our second, due just two months later! So, it can be seen from the above that, since joining the Hyperactive Children's Support Group 30 years ago, we have never looked back, and we are eternally grateful to Sally for all the help she has given in transforming our lives.

With our warmest regards,
Julia
November, 2007.

Thanks to the HACSG

My life and that of my family would be very different and much the poorer had I not made contact with Sally Bunday, her mum, Vicky Colquhoun and the HACSG in 1979.

I come from a large family and was looking forward to having children, with no apprehensions. However when my son came along, by caesarean section, he was very wakeful and cried a lot. Even in hospital he was test-weighed to ensure he was taking sufficient food - he was taking plenty!

He continued to be very fretful and slept very little, despite feeding voraciously and often. I took him to my GP, under whose direction we tried various sedatives, unsuccessfully. Finally Valium was prescribed, which made him even more wakeful. I was told that the only way to get him to sleep would be to give him a general anaesthetic each night. Obviously this was not a solution so I plodded on. There seemed to be no help available. I was getting exhausted and eventually ending up on medication myself, which included anti-depressants. I did my best to manage, however I felt like a zombie, totally out of control of my life. In reflection, unwisely, I decided to stop my medication, without gradual withdrawal or supervision. I went blind for a period of time, which was very frightening. My sight returned and whilst I was still tired and had my 'problem' child to deal with, at least I was back in control of my senses.

As my son grew he had a very short concentration span, was often unhappy, badly behaved, erratic and had many infections, rashes, hallucinations. He was a very sad little boy. He walked before he was 8 months old, because he was awake so much. At playgroup (3 years old) he was named 'mafioso' - we can laugh, but this was my dear child who had behavioural problems, was miserable, found it difficult to sit still, was accident prone, and unsurprisingly was not popular with the other Mums. Still there seemed to be no-one who could help us.

By the time he was nearly six, I had only two real friends left in the world - neither of whom had children at my son's school. People did not want to be around me or my son. One of these two friends saw an article in a magazine, the other friend heard a discussion on the radio re the connection between food and behaviour. I made contact with the HACSG and found that Sally Bunday had experienced similar difficulties with her son Miles and had found that the Feingold Diet had helped.

I thought I had been feeding him quite healthily - I was making my own home-made wholemeal bread, gave him yogurts. However, I started to read labels and avoided giving him any food or drink containing artificial additives. His behaviour changed within a day. He seemed calmer. In a week the headmistress met me in the school playground and said the change in his behaviour was a miracle and that I should write a book (I still haven't got round to it!)

My dear son became someone I had never known. Just 7 years old, my little boy volunteered: "I don't feel angry all the time any more". "I haven't got pains in my head and body any more"

Whilst prior to having my son I thought I would probably like two or maybe three children, because of his difficulties, I ensured that I didn't get pregnant. However once we saw so much improvement in his behaviour/sleeping etc. we decided to have another child, and my daughter was born.

My son had joined the cub scouts and when I picked him up one day, with my baby girl in arms, I met a lady I'd not seen for years. It was difficult for her to believe that I could have another child. She had known my son (and his behaviour!) from playgroup, and knew that I was NEVER going to have another child as he was so difficult.

Contacting the HACSG and changing his diet was the start of a new journey in our lives. The start of him being more 'normal' and us being a more 'normal' family.

His teacher recognised that he may be dyslexic, for which we were very grateful, and not surprised as his maximum concentration span was 60 seconds.

Our journey continued with him having help for his dyslexia. We also found that reducing the sugar, wheat and milk in his diet made even more improvement. It was worth it - this little boy had a normal life, was no longer a social pariah.

Just a few years ago he said to me "if you hadn't done what you did when I was young (i.e. adjusting his diet) I would probably have ended up in prison". He is now very hard working, happily married with a little boy of 18 months.

I was amazed at the difference food could make to my son, but I had also found that my health improved significantly, and also subsequently so did my daughter's eczema. The importance of food in relation to our health and wellbeing inspired me to want to share this powerful information and help others. I initially trained in nutrition and then various other complementary disciplines. So, since 1988, I have been working as a Nutrition Consultant and Holistic Therapist, doing my best to help people with a wide range of health problems.

Life hasn't been all sweetness and roses. Like all families there have been ups and downs. However, as you have read, my contact with Sally, Vicky and the HACSG changed the lives of those in my family, but especially my son, in a very positive way. I am forever grateful for the guidance and support I was given.

First of all, **Sam**. Now 19 and at Hull University reading Sports Science with Management and having a great time. I first brought him to you as the alternative was murder, as he would not sleep through the night at 3 years old, woke with screaming tantrums and was never in a good mood it seemed at all. We had never made the connection with his Dad's allergies or realised that they could be passed down the generations, so his going on the diet was a revelation to all of us. Within a week he was sleeping and the head banging on the floor stopped. We have kept him pretty much on the straight and narrow until he went to Australia last year. He still avoids chemicals and certain washing powders as they make his skin erupt, hates the detergent line in the supermarket as it smells dreadful to him, but now eats (and drinks!) pretty much what he wants. He does get bad hay fever which we think is grass and birch pollen - not much use for a cricketer! He still gets the tell tale red stripes down his face when he is having things he should not. From being so grumpy at 3 he is the most cheerful chap you could hope to meet now!

William is 16 now and in his last GCSE year. He has been the most badly affected, with the wheat, corn and rye intolerances. At least he gets no hay fever! He has had bread and pasta on prescription for years and is currently doing food tech as one GCSE option, quietly adapting the recipes to suit himself, with the teacher not being aware of this until a recent parents evening when she was fascinated. He is less stressed and obsessive than he was. We had a psychometric test done last summer showing that he had short term memory recall problems, which we knew, as the obsessive checking of facts, times etc was definitely out of the ordinary. His course work has always been As and Bs but exams were Es and Fs', not usual! In fact, he could not remember the questions having just read them. He has been awarded 25% extra time in exams and his grades have shot up to Bs and Cs. He loves his sport and is doing well at cricket and football. I dread him driving soon as he is still not the most co-ordinated child. However, he too is very happy with lots of friends.

Stephen, 13 was really the least affected. He has to avoid dairy and interestingly, too much potato will make him feel, but not usually be, sick. We all stay clear of nuts because of Charles and his peanut allergy. Stevie is artistic, very good at drama and the only one in the family who is left handed. He appears to be an A grade student at school but only when he puts his mind to it! He is not sporty like the other two but still manages to be in the hockey team and play cricket which he loves.

So, we cope. The things I have learnt over the years, are, that anything can be managed if you put your mind to it; nothing is the end of the world, as there is always a way to sort it out! Nearly all recipes can be adapted, and if children children start by eating proper food they will not want junk. Ours love food, Sam's biggest complaint at university is the standard of meals!

The funniest thing that happened regarding the boys diet was when Will went away with school for a weekend at an activity centre. I warned them about his food and that he could easily get over excited. I could tell they were thinking "stupid woman". They came back on the Sunday afternoon

as Will had slept 3 hours in 48 and talked solidly all the time he was awake!. They believed me the next time, I sent special food & he was fine. I do wish I had been a fly on the wall.

Other than that, the "switch off" (tears under the tongue) was a god send until they were old enough to be reasoned with and even then it had its uses.

I cannot believe how easy going they all are now, and it has all been worth it. It will be interesting to see the next generation but not too soon, I'm not old enough yet!

Heather

Luke

Every child has a right to a happy and carefree childhood but up to now this has been lost to my nine years old son Luke who suffers from multiple food and chemical intolerances that have seriously impaired his learning and behaviour for many years.

Luke's early months of life were very unsettled and at six months old he was placed in foster care to live with myself and my five years old daughter Claire. His development was slow, he sat up late, never learnt to crawl and his speech and understanding was delayed. Social services began a series of unsuccessful attempts to return Luke back to his birth family and the following three years were very chaotic.

At two years old Luke was very loving but he could also been very aggressive and unpredictable and visits to family and friends were stressful because without warning he would have huge screaming tantrums and break toys and he would also suddenly attack me by pulling out clumps of my hair and scratching and biting me. One close relative banned Luke from their house when he was three years old and on another occasion Luke gave my mother a black eye when he suddenly attacked her. At the time I had no idea that the food he was eating might be the cause of his Jeckyll and Hyde behaviour.

Luke also attacked other children at nursery and other parents began to complain. One day Luke injured several children and I cried because I couldn't understand why this was happening. Luke had eaten some green jelly sweets before nursery but at the time I didn't realise the significance of this. Luke's health and development was very closely monitored by health and social workers while he lived with me in foster care but nobody advised me that food could affect his behaviour and learning.

I eventually adopted Luke when he was four years old and initially he seemed to make progress but unfortunately his transfer from nursery to the local infants school went badly wrong. The school discussed Luke's case with a child psychiatrist and I was informed that ADHD had been ruled out but Luke had been diagnosed as autistic and the school advised me to send Luke to a nearby special school.

Fortunately another local mainstream school offered Luke a place with excellent support when he was six years old and this has been very successful. The child psychiatrist withdrew his diagnosis of autism and instead diagnosed Luke with an attachment disorder but he later changed his mind and said Luke had dyspraxia but this was also ruled out and eventually in November 2006 he diagnosed Luke with a learning disability and a speech and language disorder.

Luke quickly settled in his new school but he still had sudden mood swings and aggressive behaviour. I noticed that Luke often behaved very badly after having fizzy drinks and in 2004 I contacted Sally Bunday and HACSG who sent me leaflets about ADHD. I remember reading about the Feingold diet but I didn't follow this up at the time because the child psychiatrist had already ruled out ADHD and I still had no idea about the true extent of Luke's food problems.

In November 2004 Luke injured his eye in the school playground and this caused an infection that was treated with antibiotics. Soon after Luke's aggressive behaviour became far more explosive and there were a number of incidents when he injured me.

In May 2005 Luke had six serious episodes of explosive behaviour during a ten day period and a truly sickening feeling went through my body when I realised that Luke's explosive behaviour was directly linked to the sweets given out for other children's birthdays, Luke was now nearly eight years old.

I immediately telephoned Sally and we spoke for a long time on the telephone and within a few days of starting the Feingold diet Luke's mood swings improved and his very fussy autistic like behaviour disappeared. For example since he was very little Luke has greatly fussed about putting on his socks and shoes and he would often try up to a dozen times before they felt okay on his feet but within only two days on the his new diet he stopped fussing over his shoes and there was also a big improvement in his repetitive speech. Since then I have kept in regular contact with Sally and she has been enormously helpful over the past two years, in 2006 I eliminated lactose from Luke's diet and started him on fish oils and soon after his school reported that he seemed more mature in his behaviour and speech and he was able to read and write simple sentences. In December 2006 Luke won the Headteacher's award for the most improved academic achievement in his class and this would have been unthinkable even a year ago.

Other parents have said that the elimination of food additives seemed to lift a fuzzy cloud from their children's brain but for Luke it has been more like the removal of a tornado that has blighted his early childhood years and devastated normal family life for Claire and myself. Luke is now nearly 10 years old and although his behaviour and learning is improving every day he still reacts very badly when new foods are re-introduced into his diet and he also becomes very aggressive and verbally abusive if he inhales the smell of aerosol sprays such as hairspray, perfume, aftershave, floor varnish, car deicer etc. Normally Luke never swears but recently he has started to swear like a trooper whenever he has a bad reaction to food or chemicals.

During the past two years I have battled and failed to get any help from the NHS and Luke is still waiting to be seen by a specialist. Unbelievably the child psychiatrist has just discharged Luke from his caseload because he has told me that he does not deal with food related behaviour problems. He also stated that because Luke's behaviour improves through diet this means that Luke does not have ADHD because he regards ADHD as a permanent neurological condition that can only be treated by drugs. I feel sick to the stomach when I think about the many childhood years that Luke has lost to the effects of food additives and chemicals on his learning and behaviour.

A vast army of multi-disciplinary professionals from the health and social services have been involved in Luke's life since infancy yet not one person ever advised me that food could be the cause of his severe behavioural problems! The scale of ignorance among professionals is breathtaking!

Although I have never met Sally in person I regard her as a close friend and I am hugely grateful for her excellent help and advice that has helped improve Luke's behaviour and his learning beyond all expectations. Every now and then I get a glimpse of a happy and calm child whose speech and

understanding of language seems more like a typical ten year old and I am reminded of the fact that Luke is only just at the start of a very long road to recovery.
Thank you Sally and the HACSG!

Thank you Sally...

I came across your web site through a link from www.what reallyworks.co.uk and it brought memories flooding back.

My son, now thirty and a happy, successful, popular and very likeable adult, was just such a handful when he was small. I discovered the HACSG when I guess it was in its infancy. What a relief and a life line it became as I was almost at the end of my tether. I would like you to pass on to Sally Bunday my heart felt thanks for bringing sanity back into my life. To know that I was not alone and that there were solutions out there was such a relief at a time when there was just no information or support available anywhere else.

When the photocopied newsletter dropped on the mat it was a joy and comfort, filled with its good advice and suggestions: even my son's headmistress was persuaded to come around from her draconian attitude and treat him more sympathetically after reading a copy.

So, thank you Sally, and all the others who were there all that time ago. You broke new ground and gave parents hope and understanding. I owe my sanity to you.

Extracts

100% improvement in **Scott** (aged nearly 12). Wish I had tried this years ago, but I didn't know about it then. It was very difficult at first to get additive-free foods, but in the past three months the supermarkets are getting more and more additive-free foods which enables me to give everyone a more varied diet. In all this time I have not had one migraine.

My 9 year old son has not had any recurrence of eczema and is a lot calmer, my husband is calmer and happier. I certainly don't get as tense as I did before and best of all, our 5 year old son has been 100% better with his asthma and eczema. He managed to come off his inhaler. The best thing I ever did was to put everyone on an additive-free diet. Lots of my friends and family are trying it as well with very good results.

James has suffered from a rare skin condition Pityriasis Lichenoides Chronica since February, 1984. He was on one occasion a case study for leading skin specialists in the East Midlands who all agreed that there was no known cause for the condition and no cure it would eventually get better of its own accord (usually after a few months). After two years it had not improved at all but after only one month on the Feingold Diet his spots (similiar to those of chicken-pox) had all disappeared. They did re-appear briefly after drinking some Sainsbury's (artificial and colour-free) lemon squash containing the preservative E223 but soon disappeared again when we stopped using it.

Baby, 14 months old: Since reading your article we have dropped all monosodium glutamate from his diet and all fruit juices and in 3 weeks we can see an improvement we have had two nights of undisturbed sleep and to me and my husband that is heaven also his general outlook is better he doesn't cry all the time and his nightmares and sleepwalking are much less.

Girl aged 5: Before she was put on the diet she was very excitable and overactive; she had many tantrums often 1 or 2 a day, and had excessive crying sessions. She was unhappy and very bad tempered, her power of concentration was poor and her speech was bad, very muddled she has to attend speech therapy. Since starting the diet there have been vast improvements. Gone are the daily tantrums and excessive crying bouts. She has definitely slowed down to a much more normal pace and her speech has started to improve rapidly. She is now most definitely a much happier little girl and my husband, my family and I are absolutely thrilled with the most outstanding results to date.

Boy 1 year old: I have now had baby on the diet for just over two weeks. Even friends who don't see him often have commented on the difference, so I really believe this is what has been the trouble. After crying tears of relief and remorse for all the times I've screamed 'for God's sake, shut up', I am now taking a real joy and pride in my lovely son instead of loving him with gritted teeth. Last week he actually slept on three separate days till 5.30 - 6 a.m. and settled again after a drink. His concentration has improved a thousandfold etc. etc. I am so enthusiastic over this I would help anyone. I am sure that children like this are much more likely to be BATTERED as time and time again friends and relatives have said 'if he was mine I just don't know how I'd cope'. I was reaching breaking point as the smacks were getting harder and more frequent, when suddenly I read your article .....

Small boy: The diet has been duplicated and will be available at the weekly clinic. I have also given copies to other playgroup mothers. As yet it has been too early to see if they have noticed any change. It is strange but we all just thought our children were awkward, etc. My son's sleeping habits have definitely improved. Before it used to be a couple of hours here and an hour there now he will go to sleep and have five hours at a stretch, play awhile and then have another hour; this alone means a great deal to my husband and L I believe he is improving behaviour wise. His eating is very spasmodic but at least four times since starting the diet he has arrived at the meal table and eaten a proper meal. A real treat for us!!

I am writing to thank you for Dr. Feingold's diet sheet. I read of your Group in the *Mother* magazine, and although my son is not hyperactive, he does suffer from hay fever or at least he did!! I am overjoyed at his response to the diet and my husband, who suffers from the same complaint, on seeing his son's obvious improvement, started the diet too. Since then neither of them has needed anti-histamine, mentholatum or eye drops, all of which were a daily necessity. I am very grateful and inform people daily of the benefits.

Mother from West Midlands: Eight months ago I put my son on the diet. We now have a healthy, contented child who I have not had to take to the doctors for 6 months. It used to be every six weeks! I would be more than willing to give any assistance if required to the local contact.

Boy aged 8: It's like living with a different child, one I always thought was "in there" but trapped by his excruciating behaviour! Can now concentrate, tie laces, dress himself, does not scream anymore, can participate in sports (was extremely disruptive at school and very destructive at home.)

Girl aged 5: M seems to have undergone a complete change (noticeable after 1-2 months of diet). She is very careful about what she eats because reactions have caused her some distress. **We are all much happier.** Response to diet very good, appetite, sleep, co-ordination good, co-operation good, less aggressive and disruptive. More affectionate and much calmer.

Boy aged 9: Grown taller and slimmed down!! What a relief from day-to-day hassle. At last a full night's sleep. T is a different child in more ways than one. I am also fully weaned off tranquilisers, thanks to the Feingold diet.

Have found L greatly improved. Sometimes has bad days but generally is a much happier, calmer and better behaved child and is definitely less aggressive and has less temper tantrums. Thank you so much our life is a life now instead of a living hell. No one can understand unless they have been there!!

Lapses in diet result in such drastic relapses in behaviour that sceptical relatives and friends have become convinced. Have successfully recommended diet to other parents. I feel this diet has significantly helped our child. Generally S is a much nicer, happier child and has a lovely nature.

Everyone we know and school say how much better T is. A changed child.

We are both pleased with H's improvement. Didn't realise colouring in food could change a child so much.

Our child has improved beyond recognition. This time last year we had an "unteachable" daughter according to infant school, and we were worried about how she would cope in the Juniors, but since going on the 'diet' she is managing just great.

Boy aged 10 at first contact. Very hyperactive even during pregnancy. Always thirsty, impulsive and clumsy. Disruptive at school and referred to psychologist. Very poor school performance. Excellent response to EFAs: happier all round, school work better, handwriting greatly improved.

Mother writes "although you did not promise a miracle I think you have given us one".

Boy aged 10 at first contact. Impossible behaviour at home and school. Poor handwriting, memory and mathematical skills. Dramatic response to EFAs: more sensible, more relaxed, "vastly improved handwriting and astonishing improvement in mathematics" : within one term moved from the bottom of the class to the top: recently qualified as a lawyer 13 years later.

Boy aged 4 at first contact. Dry skin, always thirsty, aggressive to other children and to mother, impossible to get to sleep at night, would not eat ordinary meals. Within 2 weeks of starting EFA's stopped being thirsty, sleep and eating patterns became normal, "mother no longer used as a punch bag".

Boy first contact aged 2. A good baby while breast fed but on weaning became violent and at 20 months expelled from a toddler's group: extremely thirsty, cried incessantly and deliberately broke anything within reach: no fear of anything, constantly running into the road, rejected all mothering and cuddling. "On a day when I would have gladly have given away my little son, I wrote to HACSG and poured out my heart. It changed my life". Within 3 weeks E was a different child. Now 6 he is a happy , well adjusted child, doing well at school, with a demonstrative affectionate nature. "I feel that his childhood was saved by HACSG and I cannot begin adequately to express my gratitude".

Aged 8 years. "I am extremely happy with R now. I don't know how I got through the first year with him, it was like a nightmare. Thank you! "

Aged 2 years. "M seems to have undergone a complete change (noticeable after about 1-2 months of diet) She is very careful what she eats because reactions have caused her some distress. We are all much happier."

Remarks from HACSG Parents Reports on response to supplements of Evening Primrose Oil & Co-factors Zinc, B6, etc. More recent research finds that Fish Oil Omega3 and Evening Primrose Oil Omega 6 are more suitable .

Boy aged 5 years "Hyperactivity lessened, allergies improved. Initially took 3-4 days to show response and overall improvement was marked"

Boy aged 4 years. "Response almost immediate 3 days improvements sustained. When zinc taken out symptoms re-appeared... when zinc re-introduced, symptoms reduced again."

Boy aged 4 years. "Improvements seen after 1 week with Evening Primrose Oil. After 2 weeks in general(including diet) improved speech, concentration, co-operation and understanding. Thirst back to normal."

Boy aged 3 years. "After 1-2 months was able to eat a less restricted diet without having any noticeable effects. Eczema and asthma somewhat better. My husband and I are thrilled at what the diet has achieved and that the world is at last able to see the lovable good child which we knew was always hiding in him. Results of infractions of the diet are not now so noticeable".

Boy aged 7 years. *Gilles de Tourette Syndrome* "His tics have virtually disappeared since being on these supplements. This was noticeable in the first week. Concentration definitely improved".

Boy aged 6 years. "Much calmer, less aggressive, able to concentrate more at school... .this started after stopping his blackcurrant drinks... but continued improving after three weeks on the supplements".

Boy aged 12 years. "Calmer, concentration better, mixing better, less aggressive(verbally), happier. Before hearing about the HACSG my husband and I were heading for a breakdown. We feel that a weight has been lifted!"

Boy aged 7 years. "A great deal calmer and better able to complete school work. Teacher impressed. Overactive bowel stopped within first week"

Boy aged 7 years. "General behaviour better. Less tearful & irritable. Patch of eczema which he has had for approximately one year has almost gone completely".

Boy aged 2 years. "Goes to bed easily at night on first attempt and does not wake often in the night. We now have many uninterrupted nights. No nappyrash and seems much happier in himself."

Boy aged 5 years. "Hyperactivity lessened, eczema and asthma improved. There has been a huge improvement in school, especially with aggression."

Boy aged 10 years. "Improvement in both eczema and asthma(now off medication) School reports increase in concentration. Less frustrated."

Boy aged 8 years. "Eight-year-old catarrh problem has disappeared; constant thirst is now normal; easier to handle; less tantrums; better appetite. Diarrhoea and vomiting stopped; more colour in cheeks. Schoolwork improved on higher dose. Teacher said there had been a big improvement in school work and behaviour. Getting good marks now. The school does not know he is on Efamol and Efavite!"

On the effects of EyeQ

This is an account of the effects that EyeQ have had on my six-year-old son. He was a very restless baby who had difficulty in sleeping and I decided on a course of Cranial Osteopathy to help him settle both night and day and this seemed to have very positive results.

When he started at pre-school nursery I was told that he had difficulty in focusing on any particular activity and that he did not settle as did the other children in the group. He then started school at four years' old and continued in the same vein with the teacher reporting to me at regular intervals that, although he had the ability, he was not progressing as he should be. He had an enormous concentration problem and was always more interested in what was going on around him than the particular task he was engaged in. When reading bedtime stories to him it was always very difficult to gain his full attention.

I decided to start him on a course of EyeQ about eighteen months ago and the result was astonishing -within two weeks he was like a different child. His handwriting had improved and on speaking to his teacher I was told that she noticed an enormous improvement in his behaviour and general progress.

On one occasion when I stopped giving him the EyeQ his behaviour deteriorated very rapidly. I shall, of course, continue now with the EyeQ. Generally he can focus on something he is interested in and cannot be distracted from that project. He always seems to have one passionate interest in his life that he talks non-stop about. At the moment it is Lego!

I myself have recently embarked on a new career with quite a lot of studying and course work involved. I was finding it very difficult to motivate myself after a day's work and two children to cope with and decided to try the EyeQ myself. I had very positive results and found my concentration greatly improved within a short space of time.

An item from The Daily Telegraph, 10th Jan, 2007

"DIET & EXERCISE TRANSFORMED OUR CHILDREN"

The behaviour of children with special needs improved "significantly" with good diet, vitamin supplements & regular exercise. Parents and teachers noted a marked reduction in hyperactivity, anger & restlessness after a 7 month regime of multivitamin supplements, healthy food & physical training. The study took place at a special school in Merton, South London, supported by "Food for the Brain" charity. Instead of sugary cereals, sweetened drinks & chocolate etc. the children were given porridge for breakfast, wholemeal bread, fruit & veg etc.

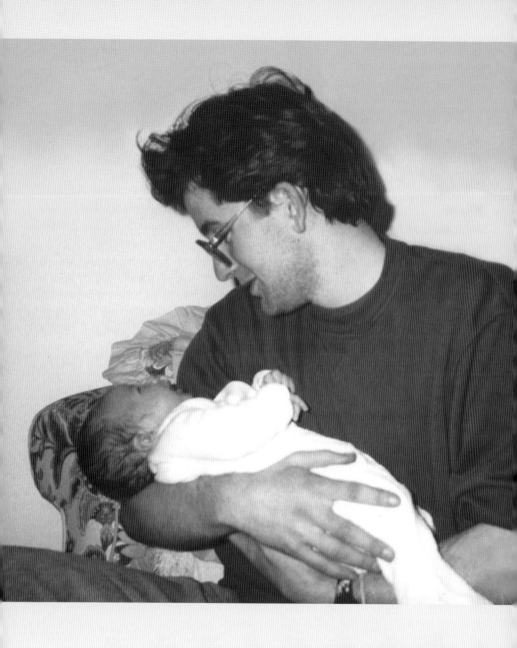

Miles with his two-week old nephew Sam

Research notes

1. *Lack of Essential Fatty Acids as a Possible Cause of Hyperactivity* S. Bunday & I. D.Colquhoun. *Medical Hypothesis*, 1981. 7:673-9.

2. *Essential Fatty Acid Metabolism in boys with ADHD*. American Journal Of Clinical Nutrition. 1995:62:761-81995 Laura Stevens *et al* of Purdue University USA carried out this research following up on the original HACSG work in 1981.

3. Dr. Alex Richardson & Dr. Basant Puri at the Department of Psychiatry, Hammersmith Hospital, carried out further research into the value of nutritional interventions for ADHD children.

4. The *HACSG Database 1987* in co-operation with Prof. Neil Ward of Surrey University, found that 357 diagnosed cases of hyperactivity responded well to food-additive restricted diets. 89% were sensitive to artificial colourings; 71% to preservatives; 59% to monosodium glutamate flavour enhancer and 48% to orange.

5. Several other studies carried out world-wide support these findings and the thirty years of work carried out by the HACSG.

6. *The Influence of Chemical Additives on the Elemental Status of Hyperactivity.* Prof.Neil Ward, Senior Lecturer in the Department of Chemistry at Surrey University in *The Journal of Nutritional Medicine*, pps. 51-5 7(1990)

7. *Disturbed Children; the Role of Food & Chemical Sensitivities*, Dr.IanMenzies, *Nutrition & Health*, Vol.3pps39-54 (1984)

8. The Asthma & Allergy Research Centre at St.Mary' s Hospital on the Isle of Wight carrying out research in 1999 found that 277 three-year-old children were adversely affected by artificial colourings & preservatives. This Study was funded by the Ministry for Agriculture, Fisheries and Food, The Food Standards Agency. *Unpublished until October 2002. The new study published September 2007 confirms these findings.*

9. In the US, a report published in November 1999 that reviewed 23 of the best studies conducted since the mid 1970s that explored links between nutrition and ADH D, concluded that the evidence strongly suggested that behavioural disorders are caused or aggravated by certain food additives. *The Center for Science in the Public Interest* urged government public health services to advise parents to try changing their childrens diets before placing them on medication such as Ritalin.

10. *The Influence of supplementary Vitamins, Minerals & Essential Fatty Acids on the anti-social behaviour of young adult prisoners* A randomised, placebo-controlled trial. C.Bernard Gesch. S.M.Hammond, Sara E.Hampson, Anita Eves & Martin Crowder. *British Journal of Psychiatry*(2002) 181.22-28

Advice to distressed parents

Distressed parents of hard-to raise children need not turn to medication to control their hyperactive children. Proper nutrition is instrumental in behaviour modification. *A short extract from Solving the Puzzle of Your Hard to Raise Child,* by the late **Dr.William G. Crook.**

In my opinion, treating the hyperactive child is like treating a person with headache or high blood pressure. In each situation, medication may temporarily relieve a person's symptoms, but should never be used on a long-term basis without attempting to identify and appropriately treat the cause. The hard-to-raise child who exhibits hyperactivity, irritability, learning problems, headaches, fatigue, depression and recurring allergies can be compared to a jigsaw puzzle with many pieces, some of them out of place. To alleviate these problems the child's parents, together with his physician, need to identify the out-of-place pieces, fit them in and solve the puzzle. Although each child is different, here are some of the most common puzzle pieces:

Poor Diet

As Vancouver physician Saul Pilar put it, if you want your child to get A-plus marks, don't give him a C-minus diet. A childs body is an amazing chemical factory and warehouse. It manufactures, processes or stores more than 100,000 different chemicals. To make these chemicals a child imports only about 50 raw materials, chemicals his body can't make by itself such as vitamins, minerals, essential fatty acids, water, glucose and fibre. If he doesn't get enough of these raw materials, his brain and body can't function optimally.

Food allergies

Observant parents and doctors have known for many years that allergies can make a child irritable and hyperactive because what a child eats could affect his behaviour. For years I've been reading articles in medical literature describing children with food-related behavioural problems. So I began to look for food reactions in my own patients and I found many youngsters whose behaviour improved when I changed their diets.

My interest in food-related disorders continued and I began to collect data on the relationship of food sensitivity to hyperactivity. After five years, I had studied and treated 182 hyperactive youngsters using elimination diets. Three out of four of the parents found their child's hyperactivity was diet related. Sugar, artificial food colours and flavours, milk, corn, chocolate, eggs and wheat were the most common offenders. Children who are tired, depressed, irritable or hyperactive could be troubled by allergy, especially allergy to foods they eat every day. "If my child eats chocolate every day", said the mother of one of my patients, "by the end of fourth day he acts so hateful you can't stay in the house with him. He can't sit still in the daytime and he rolls and bumps around in his bed at night. When I eliminate chocolate from his diet his behaviour changes. I can't believe he's the same child". Many other physicians have conducted studies like mine and reached similar conclusions. In a recent issue of The Lancet, J. Egger. M.D. and associates published a carefully designed and executed scientific study of 76 hyperactive children, 62 of whom improved on elimination diets. The most common offenders were artificial colours and preservatives, milk, chocolate, wheat, oranges, eggs and sugar.

Nutritional Supplements

A change in diet is among the most effective treatments for hyperactive children, however, dietary modifications alone may not be enough. Nutritional supplements including vitamins A, B complex, C, D and E; minerals calcium and magnesium; and trace minerals chromium and zinc have been found beneficial in treating children with behaviour problems.

For example, Welsh researchers Benton and Roberts studied 90 school children ages 12 and 13, half of whom received a nutritional supplement. According to their report in The Lancet, 8 months later those children who received the multivitamin-mineral supplements showed a 9-point increase in verbal intelligence over the non-supplemented control group.

Maryland pediatrician Arnold Brenner, M.D., noted that some of his hyperactive patients improved dramatically when he administered large doses of vitamin B-6. Yet in other children, hyperactive behaviour was accentuated. However, some of these patients improved when they were also given supplemental minerals along with vitamin B-1, B-12 and other B vitamins. Therefore, insurance doses of all vitamins should be given before increasing one vitamin alone. Mary Coleman, M.D., of Washington, demonstrated in the early 1970s that large doses of B6 raised the blood serotonin levels significantly in some hyperactive children which indicates that B6 might be as effective or more effective than Ritalin in controlling behaviour. Even for children who usually follow a well-balanced diet, supplementation often is necessary since nutrient absorption is affected by chemical sensitivity, yeast-related health problems and environmental toxins.

The late William G, Crook, M.D, received his medical education and training at the University of Virginia, the Pennsylvania Hospital and Johns Hopkins. He has authored numerous scientific articles and books including The Yeast Connection and Solving the Puzzle of Your Hard-to-Raise Child. Until his death in 1999, Dr.Crook was a firm supporter of, and friend to the HACSG.

Nutrition and childhood health and behaviour

Dr. Dorothy West MRCS. LRCP, MF Hom.

Many modern children have become hooked on processed food and are accustomed to large quantities of sugar, fat and flavourings in their diet. For instance many breakfast cereals are loaded with sugar as they have heavy sugar coating on each grain, others have more subtle sugar content. The problem is that sugar is highly addictive. One specialist wrote about her patients in a rehab clinic that her heroin addicts would find it much easier to give up their heroin than their sugar.

Many problems stem from processed foods which are high in sugar, fat and flavourings but low in vitamins and minerals. In other words we have empty calorie foods which satisfy the hunger but have little nutritional value.

Children do not have a natural love of sugar if they are brought up on an additive free low sugar diet well balanced with fruit, vegetables and protein. However they very easily acquire a taste for sugar and then demand it. One only needs to view the supermarket shelves to see how popular sweets, chocolates, cakes, biscuits and sweetened drinks are.

All foods are broken down to sugar as the basic fuel which the body burns for energy. Added refined sugar upsets the balance. Sugar requires a whole range of vitamins and minerals in order to be used in the body. B vitamins and minerals such as zinc, magnesium and manganese are essential in the process of metabolism or burning of sugar. Without these essential nutrients the body gradually runs into deficiencies.

Magnesium deficiency can cause restlessness, zinc deficiency results in impaired immune response, manganese deficiency can be implicated in depression, iron deficiency causes anaemia. Deficiency in B vitamins causes fatigue, irritability, sleeplessness and a whole host of other problems including skin rashes.

Fresh vegetables, fruit, meat and fish are loaded with vitamins, minerals, protein and unsaturated fats and provide an abundant supply for health but they need care in preparation and cooking. Even so in today's world the soil can be impoverished and a daily supplement is useful.

However, with modern eating habits, it is quite usual for a family to eat a nutritionally inadequate processed meal such as pizza or chicken nuggets and chips in front of the TV. Working mothers are hard pressed to make a meal from basic ingredients and we have a whole generation which lacks the knowhow on cooking simple meals from scratch. Inevitably children fed in this way become depleted in essential nutrients and it shows. Lack of concentration, restlessness and irrational behaviour emerge. The child becomes pale-faced with dark shadows under the eyes and very often has a runny nose or constant cough. It becomes difficult to feed such a child who has food fads often because of a zinc deficiency which dulls the sense of taste and smell. Mother gives up the fight and allows the child to choose junk rather than starve.

The way a child is affected has so many variations from bed-wetting to skin problems and educational difficulties. Obesity and diabetes are now becoming common in young children. But the response to a well-balanced diet with appropriate supplements can be very dramatic. It seems so simple as to be incontrovertible but vested interest prefers to offer drugs to deal with the many facets of nutritional deficiencies. It is all a matter of education versus vested interest.

Hidden and silent allergy

Dr. Edward C. Hamlyn, MB., ChB.

When a child has an allergy to a food, which is eaten every day, the child adapts and contains the reaction so that the allergy becomes masked. This makes the problem of allergy mysterious and difficult to understand. All sorts of things can unmask the allergy to a slight or major extent. The clinical picture is most difficult to cope with, when the allergic reaction targets the central nervous system.

The child can exhibit the Jekyll-and-Hyde syndrome. At times a little angel at other times a real devil. This personality switch is diagnostic of food allergy, but is usually thought to be some sort of mental problem. There has been an enormous increase in the incidence of allergy during the last 50 years and this is especially true of allergy in children.

A failure to understand what is happening and treating the condition as a genetically determined illness with drugs, has magnified the problem out of all proportion. Once the phenomenon is recognised and understood, drugs are never ever needed.

The source of the trouble can be spotted, taken out of the diet and normality restored. Using drugs in a vain attempt to hide the problem, makes matters worse and vastly increases the incidence of the condition. It is medical malpractice and child abuse to miss the correct diagnosis and create a drug addict. A treated case can be made incurable. That is a crime.

Nutritional Health & Offending Behaviour

"Growing Straight"

C. Peter W. Bennett

Mind the gap!

A gap exists in the criminal justice system (CJS) between what is said and what is done by the agencies within it, including education. Crime prevention is separated from criminality prevention to the detriment of restorative justice. There is a gaping failure to help offending children who are more likely to be diseased physically than being mentally ill. Another gap grows between mental and physical health in the National Health Service (NHS).

Our police have always been involved with health and disease as well as crime. In the 1880's, Manchester police superintendent Bent ran a soup kitchen for children. His chief constable stopped him but a public outcry re-instated his criminal-preventing service and expanded it to clothing provision and canal holidays. A hundred years later, this author was a police superintendent developing nutritional criminal prevention. A trial called 'The Shipley Project' demonstrated the district's most prolific young offenders had multiple physical symptoms, allergies, nutritional and biochemical disorders. When corrected through diet, nutritional supplements and medical treatment, their health, education and behaviour improved. Evidence on film was striking. Shipley Division's juvenile crime rate went down whilst increases occurred in neighbouring and comparative divisions. The chief constable stopped further work on grounds that health and diet were not a policing matter and should be left to Social Services.

One Director of Social Services admitted a statutory duty to fund special diets for needy children, but rejected the Shipley project as not scientifically or medically proven. This dismissive charge has oft been made by other CJ professionals. Perhaps they do not see the positive effects in the enlightened anthropological wood for the darkly negative sociological trees. A similar phenomenon occurs in medicine with the "placebo effect". Perhaps this blindness causes them to miss opportunities to do "what works" in real-life. Science contributes valuable objectivity but the real world needs the art of subjective application. Scientific dominance makes a casualty of empathy which arises from balanced objectivity and subjectivity. Sympathy is the unbalanced subjective element that replaces empathy.

The present government has identified several gaps needing to be filled in social welfare, education, health and criminal justice. It wants "seamless" services. The stitches in the NHS seams have burst asunder and it is forced into bed with CJS for safe intercourse under surveillance if not connivance from police! This presents an opportunity to bridge the gap between mental and physical health practices and statutory duties under Criminal Justice Acts, Children's Acts and the Police and Criminal Evidence Act (PACE). However, the police appear unaware of their potential to identify physical as well as mental health problems. The PACE Act 1984 allows police to take hair, blood, sweat and even tears in order to prove or disprove criminality. It's the 'disprove' they forget. The prime minister's popular mantra should be, "Tough on the Causes of Crime but Mind the Gap".

Filling the gap!

Hyperactive and attention disordered children often act without thought of consequences to themselves or others. They are unhappy people who make others unhappy. There are many contributory factors and rarely is there a single cause for offending or criminal behaviour. Social Services should recognise that persistent offenders and failing students have poorer health, greater malnutrition and more disrupted biochemistry than non-offenders, even within the same family sharing genetics, environment and diet such as 'Rat Boy' of recent infamy.(1) The Hyperactive Children's Support Group (HACSG) has amassed some of that evidence along with other groups, organisations, parents and individual researchers. There is a substantive case to prove the role of nutrition in criminality and other anti-social behaviours. Some evidence meets the stringent demands of the scientific medical school and the rest would satisfy a jury in a criminal trial. Some evidence appears elsewhere in this publication and contributes toward development of an integrated restorative health and restorative justice paradigm for criminality prevention. It may help also to fill the gap.

A case study

An 11-year-old boy in Suffolk had been arrested twenty times for various crimes including assaults on other boys, breaking windows and graffiti on a police cell door. Incredibly, his condition of bail was not to harass a certain police officer! His solicitor secured legal aid for assessment and expert witness evidence and persuaded the Youth Court to defer sentence for three months. The boy was excluded from school and was not receiving home tuition. He was violent and destructive at home. An assessment in June 2001 revealed:

Tachycardia with a racing and 'thumping' heart that put him in fear of dying and suicidal

High score on Conners ADHD scale but consultant psychiatrist would not diagnose ADHD, calling it a non-treatable personality disorder.

Hair analysis found deficiency in calcium, chromium, manganese and selenium; low iron, magnesium, sodium, cobalt, iodine and zinc; high toxic aluminium, cadmium and lead.

Mineral imbalances were linked to his symptoms, including irritability, fear, palpitations, nervousness, hyperactivity, uneven heart beat, indigestion, muscle and stomach cramps. Urine test indicated pyroluria (purple factor) associated with hyperactivity and inadequacy of metabolizing zinc and vitamin B6.

Allergic or intolerant to rye, lemon, lettuce, apple, codfish, cola drinks, egg, honeydew melon, onion, orange, pear, shellfish, tuna and potato.

Gut affected by the yeast, *Candida albicans,*

Reactions to food chemicals and drugs: Ammonium Chloride (510), Indigo Carmine (E132), Acid Orange (El 10), Crystal Ponceau (E124), Polysorbate 80 (E433) and Penicillin.

The boy wanted to stop getting into further trouble and he accepted a difficult dietary and nutritional supplementation regime. Social Services had encouraged his mother to put him on Ritalin but neither wanted that. Remarkably, he kept out of trouble for more than three months prior to returning to court in October, 2001. The tachycardia had all but disappeared, as had other symptoms. He was much happier and healthier and his behaviour at home was better although not perfect. The magistrates were so impressed that they imposed a supervision order without conditions and a curfew order rather than the intended and expected custodial sentence. Further hair analysis after court disposal indicated significant improvement in calcium, iron, magnesium, chromium, cobalt, iodine, manganese, selenium, vanadium and zinc. Molybdenum was unchanged but sodium and potassium were worse. Aluminium, cadmium and lead were all reduced to below threshold levels. The boy was accepted by residential private school that undertook to continue his restorative health programme.

Conclusion - closing the gap

Legal provisions to diagnose and treat physical health problems of offenders would be better met through integration of this approach. A new synthesis for preventing criminality through ecological or holistic health is possible and can be implemented efficiently, effectively, economically and environmentally. In particular, this approach meets the essential criteria of Hippocrates and the medical profession that first, it will do no harm. At worst there may no change but it is likely to produce variable but quantifiable improvements in the health, school and community life. In the light of changes in the National Health Service, particularly through partnership working between statutory and voluntary organisations, this approach is readily available to be integrated into community health improvement plans, whether the community is closed such as in prisons or open as in urban or rural settings. Semi-closed communities, such as military and police organisations, have the opportunity of leading on such integration because of their higher levels of discipline and their particular dependence and requirements for physically and mentally healthy and fit personnel.The evidence reveals there is no systematic procedure for prevention and correction of nutritional health deficiencies and there is no systematic procedure for tackling the 'whole' person in our public health, education and criminal justice institutions despite statutory requirements of Criminal Justice, Children's and Police and Criminal Evidence Acts. Legal provisions for biological sampling and analyses can be utilised to develop crime investigation into criminal prevention. This would be helpful to parents, health visitors, nurses, medical practitioners, teachers, social workers, police, probation, legal practitioners and jurists as well as politicians. Application of nutritional and biochemical assessment and the offer of treatment fits the legal requirements and can close the gap. Closing the gap will enable and empower potential and actual young offenders not only to go straight but literally to grow straight through dietary intervention and nutritional support. This would be true restorative justice.

(1)Rat Boy was a prolific offender and escaper from custody in Northumbria in early 1990s. Police and Social Services said he committed crime to feed his drug habit. In fact, he had been diagnosed hyperactive and his parents (stable marriage with other non-offending children) were persuaded to put him into care but Social Services failed. He was physically under-developed and small enough to hide or live in ventilation and drainage shafts. His drug habit developed from Valium® prescribed by his GP doctor to 'treat' his hyperactivity.

C. Peter W. Bennett BA(Hons), MA(Oxon), MBA(Aston) is a Consultant in Policing & Criminal Prevention and an Advisor to the HACSG.

The full version of this article was published in *Nutrition Practitioner* (2001) 3, 3, 48-53

Cartoon drawn for the HACSG by Pat Blake

HELP FOR
HYPER - HARRY!

For further information send SAE to:-
The Hyperactive Children's Support Group
71 Whyke Lane, Chichester,
West Sussex, PO19 2LD

MUM WAS TEARING HER HAIR OUT!

EVEN THE DOG WAS SCARED
OF HARRY!!

I'M OFF!!

MUM'S FRIENDS DIDN'T WANT HARRY
IN THEIR HOMES

I'M REALLY SORRY BUT I CAN'T STAND IT!

ONE DAY MUM WAS PACKING HARRY'S

LUNCH BOX WHEN HER SISTER, SUE,

POPPED IN FOR A CUP OF TEA.

HARRY'S MUM WAS CRYING!

I DON'T KNOW WHAT TO DO WITH HARRY!

DON'T CRY! SOME PEOPLE ARE UPSET BY THINGS THEY EAT AND IT CAN MAKE THEM BEHAVE BADLY

SUE TOLD HARRY'S MUM ALL ABOUT THE
FOODS THAT MIGHT BE BAD FOR HARRY

WE'RE CHANGING YOUR DIET, HARRY!

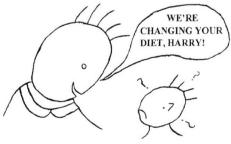

HARRY COULD **NOT** KEEP STILL!

SOMETIMES HE WAS VERY UNKIND TO HIS BABY SISTER

AT SCHOOL HE NEVER LISTENED TO HIS TEACHER AND WAS VERY NAUGHTY!

AND HE WAS ALWAYS THIRSTY!

SUE LOOKED AT HARRY'S LUNCH

IN THE BOX THERE WERE:

A HAM SANDWICH
AN ORANGE
A CHOCOLATE BISCUIT
FLAVOURED CRISPS
A BLACKCURRANT DRINK
COLOURED SWEETS

ONE OR ALL OF THESE COULD UPSET HARRY

IT WAS LIKE MAGIC!

WHEN HARRY STOPPED EATING ALL THE THINGS THAT UPSET HIM HE BECAME A MUCH NICER BOY! HE FELT BETTER, LOOKED BETTER, WORKED BETTER AND PLAYED BETTER.

NOW EVERYONE IS HAPPY!

Further vindication...of a sort

A team of American scientists carrying out the Multimodal Treatment Study of children with ADHD has found that, over a three year period, drug treatments for hyperactivity such as Ritalin and Concerta brought about no demonstrable improvement in children's behaviour although over the short term they may be of some benefit. It was also found that the drugs could stunt normal growth.

The research, the results of which were released on November 12, 2007, and shown on the BBC programme Panorama, raises important questions about the value of drug treatment in the long term. According to the Guardian newspaper, GPs in Britain prescribed Ritalin and other drugs to around 55,000 children in 2006. The HACSG has been consistently of the opinion that treating the symptoms of this disorder with medication provides no long term solution and may in fact, as this new study has shown, do more harm than good. For some time now, especially in the US where the use of Ritalin and other medication in the treatment of ADHD has become almost routine, there has been growing opposition to the use of these drugs the use of which presents, it is claimed, very serious long term health risks.

Professor William Pelham, of the University of Buffalo, commented that he thought the beneficial effects of medication had been exaggerated after the first studies were done in the 1990s. The new study, he said, had shown that the beneficial effects were none, and that the children suffered a substantial decrease in their rate of growth. "In the short term medication will help the child behave better", commented Professor Pelham, "in the long term it won't. And that information should be made very clear to parents."

Dr. Kendall, of the Royal College of Psychiatrists, who is helping to draw up the new NHS guidelines for the treatment of ADHD, commented that doctors" have reached the point where they don't know what else to offer".

He went on to say that he hoped they would be able to make recommendations that will give people a "comprehensive approach to treatment and that will advise about what teachers might be able to do within the classroom when they're trying to deal with kids who have difficult problems of this kind. I think the important thing is we have a comprehensive approach that doesn't focus on just one type of treatment".

Could that "comprehensive approach" perhaps include a look at the nutritional status of ADHD children and the control of their diet? Or will the medical profession continue to ignore the evidence of the short and long term benefits of the dietary approach to ADHD, which, *at the very least*, does not compromise the normal physical development of children?

with acknowledgements to The Guardian report, Monday, November 12, 2007.

The Hyperactive Children's Support Group

If you would like a copy of the free **Introductory Pack**, please send two 1st Class stamps to: HACSG, 71 Whyke Lane, Chichester, West Sussex, PO19 7PD, United Kingdom.
email : hyperactive@hacsq.org.uk
Website : www.hacsg.org.uk

Other HACSG publications of interest include:

ADHD: The Dietary/Nutritional Approach.
A Summary of Research
by Irene Colquhoun and Sally Bunday MBE, co-founders of the HACSG.

For the student or professional who needs to know more about the dietary and nutritional approach , this summary is essential. It lays out clearly the research upon which the approach of the HACSG is based, along with the sources. Available from the HACSG only price 5.00 including postage. (UK only).

Essential Fatty Acids, Minerals & Vitamins and their importance in the management of ADHD/Hyperactivity.
A collection of documents and case studies that help us to understand the role of the EFAs and vitamin/mineral supplements in the treatment of ADHD/Hyperactivity. Available only from the HACSG, price 5.00, including postage.(UK only)

HACSG Guide For Parents
The Guide, which is free with membership, includes the Feingold Food Programme, the day to day dietary needs of the ADHD child, foods and drinks to be avoided; food additives to be avoided, etc. Another chapter offers some suggestions for meals and also the food allergies that may contribute to a child's hyperactive behaviour. The whole family can benefit from the advice given in this book. Available only from the HACSG, price 7.00 (incl.postage in UK)